500 Classroom Tips
Grades 2-3

500 Classroom Tips
Grades 2-3

About This Book

Looking for creative ideas to get organized and add some fresh appeal to your classroom routines? We've got 500 of them just for you! Whether you are a first-year or seasoned teacher, this idea-packed resource is your guide to creating and maintaining a motivating and productive classroom. We've collected the best classroom-tested ideas from *The Mailbox*® magazine and conveniently organized them into one comprehensive package. Inside you'll quickly and easily find surefire suggestions on the timely topics you need most!

- Classroom Routines and Events
- Organizational Tips
- Curriculum Ties and Lesson Helps
- Student Motivation and Work Management
- Communications

Managing Editor: Cindy Daoust

Editorial Team: Becky S. Andrews, Kimberley Bruck, Karen P. Shelton, Diane Badden, Susan Walker, Karen A. Brudnak, Sarah Hamblet, Hope Rodgers, Dorothy C. McKinney

Production Team: Lisa K. Pitts, Pam Crane, Clevell Harris, Rebecca Saunders, Jennifer Tipton Bennett, Chris Curry, Theresa Lewis Goode, Ivy L. Koonce, Clint Moore, Greg D. Rieves, Barry Slate, Donna K. Teal, Tazmen Carlisle, Amy Kirtley-Hill, Kristy Parton, Debbie Shoffner, Cathy Edwards Simrell, Lynette Dickerson, Mark Rainey, Cathy Spangler Bruce

www.themailbox.com

©2004 by THE EDUCATION CENTER, INC.
All rights reserved.
ISBN# 1-56234-597-4

Manufactured in the United States
10 9 8 7 6 5 4 3 2

Classroom Routines and Events

Contents

Attendance

Attendance at a Glance

Here's a quick and interactive way to take attendance! Display a poster board chart, like the one shown, in an easily accessible location. Use a wipe-off marker to write a yes/no question on a laminated sentence strip; then mount the strip above the chart. Place a basket containing one personalized clothespin per student near the display. A student enters the room, reads the question, and indicates her answer by clipping her clothespin on the appropriate side of the chart. A quick glance in the basket reveals which students are absent. At the end of the day, return all clothespins to the basket and reprogram the sentence strip with another yes/no question. Now that's a wonderful way to start the day!

Karen M. Moser
Wells Elementary
Plano, TX

Roll Call

Break the monotony of checking classroom attendance and make it a learning experience at the same time. Instead of answering "here" or "present," have students answer with their birthdate, address, or phone number. Be sure to have the information handy to help children with their answers. This adds a little variety, and is an excellent way for children to review important information.

Linda Tankersley, San Antonio, TX

Double Duty

Take morning attendance *and* size up how students are feeling! Label six brightly colored rectangles with words that convey a mood or feeling, such as *happy, sad, worried, excited, angry,* and *confused.* Post the signs and provide a container of clothespins personalized for your students. Each morning a child clips his clothespin on the rectangle that best describes his mood. A quick glance in the container establishes who is absent. And a quick survey of the rectangles reveals the temperaments of those who are present. Increase student vocabulary by displaying a new assortment of word cards each month.

Julie Snyder—Gr. 2
Fair Grove Elementary School
Thomasville, NC

Student Attendance

You'll never have to take attendance again with this system! Make a poster board chart with a pocket for each child's name. Place the chart near the door. In the morning when children come in, they remove their name cards and place them in the "I'm Here!" basket. Names left on the chart show you at a glance who's not present.

Lisa Swazey
Tucson, AZ

Attendance Incentives

This idea will improve the daily attendance of your classroom. Draw an ice-cream cone on your chalkboard. Add one scoop of ice cream to the drawing when all children are present for one day. At the end of three weeks, award the class two minutes of free time for each ice cream scoop they have earned. Try adding length to a worm or a ladder, birds to a tree, eyes to a monster, eggs to a basket, and spots to a dog.

Rebecca L. Gibson, Auburn, AL

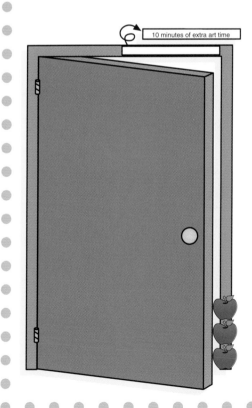

Perfect Attendance

Encourage perfect attendance with this easy-to-make display. Label a construction paper strip with a classroom privilege (such as ten minutes of extra art time). Attach the strip, facedown, to the top of a door casing. Laminate several cutouts of a shape. Each day perfect attendance is achieved, attach a cutout to the door casing. Work from the bottom to the top of the casing. When the cutouts equal the height of the paper strip, reveal the hidden reward.

Rebecca L. Gibson
Auburn, AL

Cheery Chart

Taking attendance is a snap with this cheery chart! Visually divide a sheet of poster board to suit your needs and make a supply of happy face cutouts. Laminate the chart and cutouts. For easy reprogramming, tape name cards in place. Attach Velcro dots to the chart and to the backs of the cutouts. Display the chart and then store the cutouts in a container nearby. Each morning, a student adds a happy face to the chart to show that she's present. Each day before dismissal, a volunteer returns the cutouts to the container. If desired, supply special cutouts for students to use when they leave the room for bathroom breaks or special classes.

Kathleen Gillin—Gr. 2
Cold Spring School
Doylestown, PA

Jared	Adriana	Jace	Gina	Jordan
☺	○	○	○	○
Cecilia	Nicholas	Matthew	Cohen	Thomas
○	○	☺	○	○
Gregory	Stephanie	Alexander	Amelia	Sonya
○	☺	○	☺	○
Patrick	Tyler	Austin		
○	○	☺	○	○

Student Information Log

Keep track of daily information using this timesaving log. On the last page of a legal-size pad, list the names of your students in the left margin. Then cut away the left margin of each remaining page to reveal the list of student names. Each day, date a blank page of the pad and record desired information (such as attendance, behavior, or skill performance) beside the appropriate student names.

Oct. 18, 2004

Stephen
Bobby
Mariah
Heather
Tambra
Connie
Tricia
Matt
Jennifer

Angel Bentley—Gr. 2
Auburn Elementary
Auburn, GA

Good Morning!

Each morning do you find yourself reminding students to complete the same four or five tasks in order to prepare for the school day? Creating a class set of "Good Morning" cards may be just what you need! Design a card like the one shown that includes a good-morning message, a list of tasks, and a colorful sticker. Make a class set of cards; then use clear Con-Tact covering to attach one card to each child's desktop. These nifty reminders will help students get off to a great start each morning!

Nancy Lyde
Kiker Elementary School
Austin, TX

Good Morning and Welcome to a Great New Day!

Is your...
1. pencil sharpened?
2. homework ready to check?
3. snack at your desk?
4. heading on your paper?
5. warm-up paper ready?

Signing Out and In

This classroom checkout system is a timesaver and a teaching tool. Each morning post a daily sign-out sheet like the one shown. When a student needs to leave the classroom, she signs the sheet and records the time. Then, when she returns to the classroom, she records the current time. You'll spend fewer minutes monitoring the classroom door, and your students' time-telling skills are sure to improve. As an added bonus, you have documentation of the frequency in which students exit the classroom.

Sue Lorey
Arlington Heights, IL

What's the Time?

Name	Out	In
Katie	8:30	8:34
Ben	8:52	8:57
Caroline	9:15	9:21
Danielle	9:30	9:36
Nicholas	10:06	10:11
Stacie	10:10	8:14

Absent Folders

Use these colorful file folders to organize work for students who are absent. Label each of several folders "Absent Folder"; then write a cheery message on each one. Laminate the folders for durability; then store them in a convenient location. When a student is absent, place an "Absent Folder" on his desk. Ask a student helper to place the absent student's assignments in the folder throughout the day. When a parent or sibling comes to retrieve the student's work, or when the student returns to school, the missed assignments are in one handy location.

Tricia Peña—Gr. 3
Acacia Elementary
Vail, AZ

Absent Folder

You Were Missed!

Sorry We Missed You!

This handy hanger will end confusion about your class's whereabouts. In advance, purchase a small slate from a craft store. Use a white paint pen to program the slate with the names of classes or activities that are held outside your classroom. To make a hanger for the slate, cut a length of ribbon; then hot-glue it to the back of the slate. When leaving the classroom, clip a spring-type clothespin next to the event or activity that indicates where your students will be; then hang the slate on your doorknob for easy viewing.

Cheryl Hall
Harbins Elementary
Dacula, GA

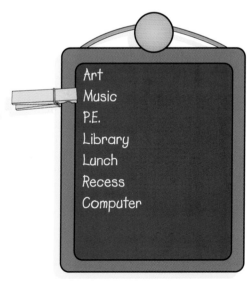

Art
Music
P.E.
Library
Lunch
Recess
Computer

Birthdays

Remembering Birthdays

At the beginning of the year, I put each child's name and birthdate in a bag with that month's calendar pieces. When I get ready to put up the calendar, I will be reminded which birthdays are in that month. I also make a dozen cupcakes at a time and store them in the school freezer. On the morning of a child's birthday, I take one cupcake out and it is thawed in time for his lunch.

Becky Williams, Roanoke, VA

Happy Birthday to You

With all that you have to do in a day, remembering your students' birthdays can be a challenge. If you utilize a little spare time this summer, you will be ahead of the game. As you relax, fill out a class set of birthday cards with best wishes and your signature. In the fall, when you learn the names of your students, address the envelopes. Organize the cards by month. Now that you are so well prepared, you will really feel like celebrating.

Mary Dinneen—Gr. 2, Mountain View School, Bristol, CT

Picture-Perfect Birthdays

Student photographs make this monthly display a kid-pleasing favorite! To prepare, take and develop a photograph of each student. Label the back of each photograph with the child's birthdate. (If the child has a summer birthday, also write the date of his half birthday and plan to recognize him in the corresponding month.) Store the photographs in envelopes by month for easy retrieval. Divide a poster-size tagboard rectangle as shown. Add a title and decorations; then laminate it. Display the resulting poster in a prominent classroom location.

At the beginning of each month, use a wipe-off marker to program the poster. Add the photographs of the students who celebrate birthdays that month and label each photograph with the appropriate date. Direct students' attention to the display and lead the class in a birthday song for the honored youngsters. At the end of the month, remove the photographs and present them to the appropriate students.

Pat Rigueira—Gr. 3, Southern Cross School, Buenos Aires, Argentina

Make-a-Wish Book

Spread birthday cheer with a class book! To keep the details of the book a surprise for the birthday child, have the youngster visit the school library or another suitable location while the rest of the class prepares the book. Invite students to brainstorm things the birthday child likes. Then give each student a copy of the form on page 55.

The student writes the birthday child's name where indicated and writes a wish that reflects the child's interests. She illustrates her work in the provided space, colors the rest of the form as desired, and signs her name on the gift tag. She glues the completed form onto a 6" x 9" piece of construction paper. Collect the resulting pages and bind them between construction paper covers. After the birthday child returns to the classroom, present him with the book of wishes. What a thoughtful gift!

Michele Culver—Gr. 2, Altamonte Elementary School
Altamonte Springs, FL

Greetings Galore

No doubt this oversized greeting card will delight its recipient! A day or two before a student's birthday, fold an 18" x 24" piece of white bulletin board paper in half to make a card. Place the card in a center stocked with crayons and markers. For message-writing inspiration, provide a list of student-generated birthday greetings or a supply of recycled birthday cards. Arrange for each child to visit the center. Have him copy a greeting, write an original message, or draw an illustration on the card. Then ask him to sign his name. Invite a student volunteer to decorate the front of the card to complete this memorable keepsake.

adapted from an idea by Gina Reagan—Gr. 3
Summerfield Elementary, Summerfield, NC

Guests of Honor

What's on the menu? Monthly birthday celebrations! Designate one day each month for lunch with birthday students and one day at the end of the year for lunch with students who have summer birthdays. Distribute invitations to the honored youngsters. Arrange to eat with your guests at a cafeteria or classroom table that you have decorated for the occasion. If desired, bring in cupcakes for a special dessert. During lunch invite each student to talk about her special day!

Jennifer Farrand
St. Thomas the Apostle School
West Hartford, CT

Classroom Jobs

Special Helpers

Choose student helpers for last-minute jobs with this simple method. Personalize a craft stick for each of your students; then place the craft sticks in a container on your desk. When a helper is needed, choose a stick from the container. Band together the sticks of those students who have already been chosen to ensure the participation of all children.

Heather Gabso—Gr. 2
Calusa Elementary
Boca Raton, FL

Helper of the Day

If you have difficulty keeping your classroom helper chart current due to frequent changes in your student enrollment, consider this idea. List your students' names in a column at one end of a magnetic chalkboard. Each day position a colorful magnet alongside the helper of the day. For convenience, begin with the name at the top of the list and move the magnet down, one name per day. Students' names can easily be added to or deleted from the list.

LuEtta Culp—Gr. 2, Louis B. Russell #48, Indianapolis, IN

Table Captains

I keep my classroom organized by appointing a different table captain each week. Table captains are responsible for keeping the table clean, passing out work, and passing out snacks. This practice helps students develop responsibility and overcome shyness.

At the end of each week, I reward table captains for their hard work. I put several different styles of pencils in a paper sack and allow each captain to select one pencil. The students love the recognition and are pleased with their gift.

Pamela Myhowich
Selah, WA

Helping Hands

If you cluster your students' desks, here's a handy way to designate weekly group helpers. Attach a colorful hand cutout (laminated for durability) to the back of one chair in each group. This child becomes his group's helper for the week. His responsibilities might include distributing and collecting papers, student folders, and math manipulatives, and keeping his group's area neat and tidy. After one week transfer each cutout to a different group member's chair. Continue in this manner until each group member has been a helper; then repeat the rotation.

Nicole Lomax, Smitsh Primary, Smiths, AL

Leader for the Day

Try this fun alternative to a weekly helper display! Create a fabric or felt chair cover like the one shown (be sure to label both sides). Each day select a classroom leader by slipping the cover over the back of a student's chair. The classroom leader becomes the line leader, paper passer, messenger, and all-around teacher's assistant for the day. At the end of the day, transfer the chair cover to the back of another student's chair. If desired, select the leaders in alphabetical order. Each student will eagerly anticipate her turn as classroom leader, and you'll be boosting self-esteems and reinforcing alphabetizing skills!

Margarett Mendenhall, Mary Feeser Elementary School, Elkhart, IN

Super Person

Here's a great way to choose your daily classroom helper. Display an apple cutout in your room labeled "Super Person!" Also ask each child to bring a recent photograph of himself to school. Stack the photographs in a desk drawer. Each morning attach the top photograph (in the stack) to the cutout. The featured child becomes the classroom helper for the day and is responsible for performing tasks such as running errands and distributing papers. At the end of the day, remove the photograph from the cutout and place it at the bottom of the photograph stack. Simple and efficient!

Lee Nelson—Gr. 2
Rural Point Elementary
Mechanicsville, VA

Classroom Jobs

Timekeeper

Just in time—a great idea for managing student sharing sessions! Each day set aside time for a predetermined number of students to share their "egg-citing" news. Ask the timekeeper to display an hourglass egg timer; then, as each student starts to share his news with the class, have the timekeeper invert the timer. If the sand in the timer runs out before the youngster is finished, the timekeeper informs him that his sharing time is over and asks him to wrap up his story. Before you know it, students will be summarizing their stories so that they can make the most of their sharing sessions.

Judith Casey—Grs. K–4, Substitute Teacher
Chatham School District
Chatham, NJ

Crate Captain

Lining students up from recess can be hectic, especially at the beginning of the year when students are not yet familiar with their classmates. Keep your students in the right spot with this great idea. Assign a crate captain to take a colorful, weatherproof crate outside for recess. Encourage youngsters to place play equipment, toys or clothing items that are not being used in the crate. Have students line up behind the crate when recess ends. Then have the captain pick up the crate as he walks to the classroom. Not only will your youngsters get back to the right room, but so will all of their belongings.

Ellen Bieleski, Elk Lake School, Dimock, PA

Equipment Manager

Assign an equipment manager to make sure youngsters have equal opportunities to use playground equipment such as rubber balls and jump ropes. Help the manager label each piece of equipment; then label class rosters to match. As children use the equipment, have them cross off their names on the appropriate class rosters. When all of the names have been crossed off a list, ask the manager to post a new roster.

Mary Dinneen—Gr. 2
Mountain View School
Bristol, CT

Jump Rope With Red Handles
Seth Goodman
~~Katie O'Neil~~
Charles Bruce
Maria Garcia
~~Henry James~~
Becca Clay
~~Derrick Watkins~~

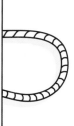

Musical Cleanup

Spruce up your classroom in no time with this upbeat game. During cleanup time, play a lively record or tape. Periodically stop the music and have students freeze. After a few seconds, resume the music and have students continue the cleanup. This musical twist adds fun to an often tiresome task, and the results will be dazzling!

Kim Schultze
Olney Elementary
Olney, MD

A Calm Way to End the Day?

How do you keep 25 excited students quiet as they wait for their buses to be called at the end of the day? Have a sharing time after students clean up their area. After the room has been straightened and the children are quiet, one child is allowed to sit in the teacher's chair and share his topic with the class. Because students *always* have something to share, this activity really helps end the day on a calm note.

Susan Valenti
Emmitsburg, MD

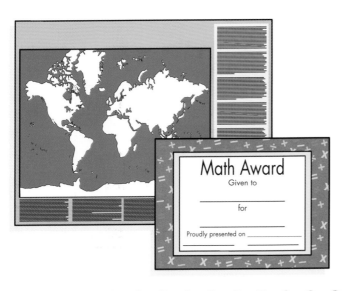

Classroom Closeout

Starting with the first school day in June, I begin taking down classroom posters, charts, displays, and learning centers. Each day after the students leave, I put away one item. The following morning, the students guess what item is missing. The student with the correct guess receives an award, often an old poster or leftover award. This method is fun for the students and a timesaver for me.

Julie Renkes
Hutchinson, MN

Foreign Language Counting

Often, to hurry my students in clearing their desks or getting out textbooks, I use the standard system of counting: One, two, three. To make it interesting, though, I count in French or Spanish. Not only do the children complete the task quickly, but they enjoy counting along with me. Later on, I count in a different language. What a great way to learn bits of other languages while performing routine classroom tasks!

Martha Ann Davis
Oakland Elementary
Greenwood, SC

You've Got
the Magic Touch!

Your desk looks spectacular!

Congratulations!

Ashley

The Clean Desk Fairy

Unannounced visits from the clean desk fairy promote orderly student desks. Make several construction paper copies of the award on page 56. Periodically distribute the awards. Attach a small surprise—such as a sticker, a pencil, or a bookmark—to each personalized award. Because the clean desk fairy arrives unannounced, students are motivated to keep their desks neat at all times. Prepare seasonal variations of the award, if desired.

Sharon Hayden
Perryville, MO

Neat Nest Award

Children will try harder to keep their desks neat when they know they may win the weekly Neat Nest Award. Make a cutout birdhouse from heavy tagboard and laminate it. Choose a different student each week to receive the award. The award may be attached to the student's desk for a week of recognition that's worth chirping about!

Connie Hamlin
Sweeny TX

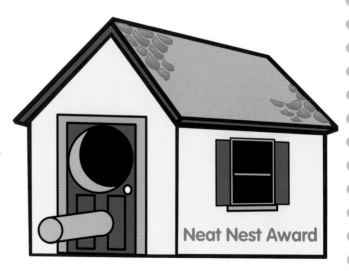

Neat Nest Award

Awesome Art Mats

These awesome art mats make cleanup as easy as 1, 2, 3! Have each student personalize and decorate an 18" x 24" sheet of construction paper. Laminate the paper mats and store them in an accessible area. Before your next art activity, pass out the mats and have students place them on top of their desks. When it is time for cleanup, simply wipe the mats with a damp paper towel or rinse them in the sink. What an easy way to keep desks clean!

Melinda Casida
Crowly Elementary
Visalia, CA

Cleanup Crew

Eliminate the daily mess that's left behind at centers by designating a cleanup crew each week. When center time is over, the crew quietly straightens each center. Your room will stay neat and tidy, and proper storage will prolong the life of your materials.

Hope Whitfield—Gr. 3, Hephzibah Elementary School, Hephzibah, GA

Hot Potato Cleanup

For a fast cleanup after a messy art project, play this version of Hot Potato. Dampen a brown paper towel or washcloth with warm water; then ball it up to resemble a potato. Have each student quickly wipe off his desktop using the hot potato before passing it on to the next student. The last student to use the hot potato places it in the trash can or in the sink to be rinsed out. This fast-paced game makes cleanup a snap!

Michele G. Curlings—Art Instructor
Colerain Elementary
Colerain, NC

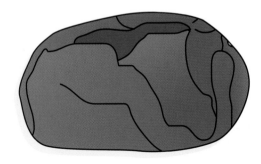

Cleanup

Magic Scrap Time

A little help from a magic scrap and poof—the classroom's all clean! In advance tell students that they will be searching for a magic scrap during cleanup time. The magic scrap can be anything that is on the floor, such as a scrap of paper, a puzzle piece, or a pencil. Before cleanup time, secretly identify a student to be the finder of the magic scrap. During cleanup time, watch that student closely and make a mental note of one item that he picks up. That item is the magic scrap. Then, when cleanup time is over, announce the identity of the magic scrap and reward the finder with a sticker. Keep a record so that all students have a chance to find a magic scrap. It works like magic!

Pat Jakubek
Terra Linda Elementary
Beaverton, OR

Neatness Counts

Tidy desks are the norm when daily desk checks become part of your routine. A few minutes before end-of-the-day dismissal, announce the impending desk check. When a child has straightened the inside of his desk and has tidied the floor space around it, he stands and waits quietly. A quick nod or verbal okay indicates to a child that he may gather his belongings and wait quietly in a designated location for dismissal. Since a clean desk is the ticket to dismissal, students quickly learn that keeping their areas neat throughout the day leaves less tidying to do at the day's end.

Ruth Watson—Gr. 2, Field Elementary School, Littleton, CO

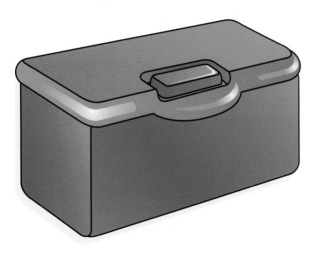

Wonderful Wipes

This tip makes classroom cleanup a breeze! In a note to parents, request that each student bring a container of baby wipes to school. Leave one container in a location that is easily accessible to students and store the rest of the containers for later use. You and your students will discover that baby wipes are especially handy for cleaning desktops, tabletops, chalk ledges, overhead transparencies, and sticky hands. As an added bonus, you'll have the freshest-smelling room around!

Laura Peter—Gr. 3
Our Lady of the Rosary
Cincinnati, OH

Names Assured

You'll never have another USP (unidentified student paper) again with this idea. Prior to collecting students' assignments say, "If your name is on your paper, draw a valentine heart (or other simple object) beside it." Since students like to draw, you can rest assured their names will be on their papers!

Sherry Gurka
Montgomery Elementary
Montgomery, TX

Magic Numbers

As each child enters my class for the first time, he is given a magic number. This number is used when textbooks are issued and throughout the year on permission slips, report cards, and other papers that must be returned. A quick check of papers will tell which ones are missing. It is easy to check papers, record grades, and file tests because the papers are always in order. We even play games, line up, and move to centers using magic numbers.

Arlene Johnston—Gr. 3, Bradenton, FL

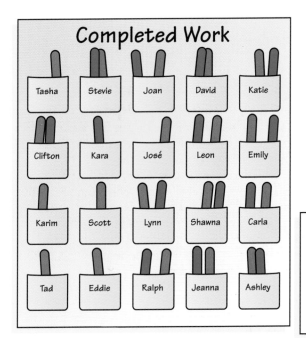

A Colorful Finish

Keep track of completed student work with a pocket chart and color-coded craft sticks. To make the pocket chart, personalize a library-card pocket for each student. Glue the pockets to a sheet of poster board that you've titled "Completed Work." Make a color code like the one shown that lists subject areas. Display the chart and the color code in a prominent classroom location. Near the chart, store a class supply of craft sticks for each color listed on the code. When a students hands in her work, she places the appropriately colored stick in her personalized pocket. A quick glance at the chart will reveal which students are still working on an assignment.

Color Code
Reading
Spelling
Math
Social Studies
Science

Cheri Loy—Gr. 2
Woodbury School
Sandwich, IL

Collecting Work

Classwork Organizer

Students do the organizing for you with this quick trick! Label several boxes for subject or skill areas you're covering. Each day, place work assignments beside the corresponding boxes. Attach a number to each box to show which assignment needs to be done first, second, and third. When a student finishes his paper, he places it in the correct box and moves on to the next number. At the end of the day, the papers are already sorted and ready for grading.

Janice M. Thames
Maxwell Elementary
Thomson, GA

Collecting Student Work

Reinforce your youngsters' alphabetizing skills and save yourself precious minutes with this collection tip. Instead of randomly collecting completed work, have an alphabetical pickup. To do this, have students bring their papers to you in alphabetical order. After you've graded the papers, you can quickly transfer the students' scores into your alphabetized grade book. And if you file your youngsters' work in alphabetized student folders, filing the papers is also a snap!

Catherine L. Nelson—Gr. 3, Edisto Primary School, Cordova, SC

Tracking Late Assignments

Keeping track of incomplete or missing assignments can be very time consuming. Enlist your students' help to make your record keeping more efficient. Keep a stack of index cards handy. Each time a student has a late assignment, he labels an index card with his name, the date, the assignment, and the reason the assignment is overdue; then he turns in the card. Once a day flip through the late-assignment cards to check on each student's progress. When a student turns in a late assignment, write the date on the corresponding card along with performance comments. File the cards by student name. The resulting card file is a handy record of each student's work habits, and it is a tremendous help when planning for parent conferences!

Charlene Fabian—Gr. 3
St. Columbkille School
Parma, OH

Alex
November 16
Math

My assignment is late because I was sick yesterday.

Individualized Assistance

Take a tip from your local baker when devising a plan for meeting with individual students. Hole-punch a class set of index cards and number them consecutively. Place the cards in numerical order on a hook attached to the front of your desk. A student seeking your assistance takes a number, knowing she'll have your undivided attention when her number is called. Or distribute numbers to those students you wish to meet with to provide instruction, encouragement, or positive feedback. Next!

Carol Ann Perks, Gifted Grs. 1–5
Comstock Elementary
Miami, FL

Paperwork Baskets

This timesaving tip helps the school day start smoothly! Rather than gathering assorted paperwork from students as you greet them each morning, ask youngsters to place the papers they have for you in a designated basket. Or go a step further and have them sort the paperwork into individual baskets labeled with specific categories, such as "Notes From Parents," "Homework," and "Permission Slips." Then, as time allows, address the paperwork in order of importance.

Barby Punzone—Gr. 3, Public School 205, Brooklyn, NY

Absent Folders

Here's a "grape" way to keep track of a student's make-up work. Sign a copy of the assignment sheet on page 57; then duplicate it. Store the copies in a convenient classroom location. When a student is absent, write his name and the date on a copy of the assignment sheet. Throughout the day, write in the appropriate space on the sheet each assignment that needs to be made up. Put the programmed sheet into a colorful folder and set it on the student's desk. When the student returns to school, he completes the assignments he missed. When he finishes an assignment, he checks it off his assignment sheet, and then he places his completed work in the colorful folder. When his make-up work is completed, he returns the folder, along with the assignment sheet, to you. If desired, request that the student's parents review the make-up work and then sign the assignment sheet.

Shannon Berry—Gr. 2
Algoma Christian School
Kent City, MI

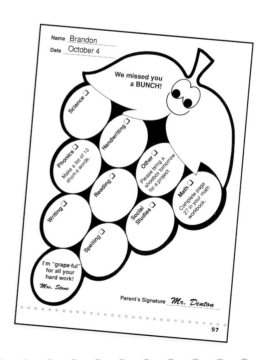

Collecting Work

Desk Pockets

Help students stay organized with colorful desk pockets. To create a class set of pockets, personalize a file folder for each student. Keeping the folders folded, laminate each one. Trim away the laminating film, leaving a ¼-inch margin. To convert each folder into a pocket, use an X-acto knife to slit the laminating film. Then attach each student's folder to her desk with a strip of clear Con-Tact paper or packing tape. Ask students to keep unfinished work in their pockets. At the end of the day, any papers remaining in the pockets are taken home as home-work. The colorful folders are also a nifty place for students to display their sticker collections.

Robin Polson-Avra—Gr. 2
New Caney Elementary
New Caney, TX

Passing the Magnets

Determining which children collect the completed assignments at the end of an activity is a cinch using this simple system. To begin, attach a decorative magnet to one desk in each row or group. The children who have magnets attached to their desks collect the assignments at hand. After placing the assignments in a designated location, each helper removes the magnet from his desk and attaches it to the desk of another student in his row or group. (In advance, establish a pre-determined route for passing the magnet in each row or group.) The next time an assignment needs to be collected, these youngsters will be in charge. Students continue passing the magnets in this manner day after day. It's fun, and it's fair!

Brenda King, Reed Elementary, Georgetown, OH

Communicate With Checkers

Here's a silent way for students to signal for your assistance. Have each child store a checker in his desk. When the student needs assistance during a quiet working time, he simply places his checker on a corner of his desk. You'll quickly get the signal, and the remainder of the group can continue working undisturbed.

Diane Fortunato—Gr. 2
Carteret School
Bloomfield, NY

Paper Collection

Review cardinal directions with your students while collecting class assignments. Have your students pass their papers to you by following your oral directions. Use directions such as "Pass all papers to the north. Now pass all papers to the east." Continue giving directions until all papers end up in your hands.

Gina Parisi—Gr. 2
Demarest School
Union, NJ

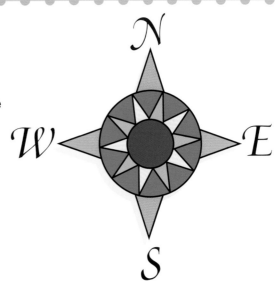

Family Matters

Minimize the problem of nameless assignments with this proven method. Arrange your students' desks into groups called families. After daily assignments are distributed, family members encourage one another to write their names on their papers. After a designated amount of time, each family that has completed this task earns a point. Reward each family after it earns a predetermined number of points.

Penny Blazer, Penns Valley School District, Spring Mills, PA

Organizing Student Work

Here's an effective way to minimize paperwork and stay organized! Label a folder for each student; then number each youngster's folder to match his listing in your grade book. During the day, have students place their completed work inside their folders. At the end of the day, collect the folders in numerical order. Grade the folders in this order so that student scores can easily be recorded in your grade book. In addition, any graded papers you wish to place in student files will also be in alphabetical order. If desired, leave graded work that is to be taken home inside the folders. As soon as the folders are distributed the following morning, students can review their work from the previous day, then place it in their cubbies for safekeeping.

Allison Dubson
North Miami Elementary
Miami Beach, FL

Conferences

The Right Place, the Right Time

To help reassure busy parents that they are indeed at the right place at the right time, post a conference schedule on your classroom door. When parents arrive, they can confirm their appointment time and relax and enjoy the preconference activities you've planned.

Julie Gockley
Ephrata, PA

Ms. Gockley's Conferences Thursday, Oct. 20	
Time	Family of
9:00	John Smith
9:15	Gail Jones
9:30	Sarah Arnold
9:45	Eddie Black
10:00	Helen Couch

Straight From the Source

In preparation for conferences, have each student write a letter to her parent(s) regarding her progress in school. Ask each child to write what she believes she has learned so far, what she has especially enjoyed learning, and what her individual goals are for improvement. During the youngster's conference, share this information with her parents. This self-appraisal will add new depth to many of your conferences.

Jennae Snow, West Elementary, St. George, UT

Homework for Parents

Here's a great way to let your students' parents know that you value their input and that you are eager to address their concerns. Several school days prior to conferences, send home a parent homework assignment like the one on page 58. When each assignment is returned, review and make a note of comments and concerns to discuss with this parent. Begin each conference by addressing the parent's comments. Your youngsters will get a kick out of the idea of homework for parents!

Joan Fate
Whittier School
Clinton, IA

I am a girl. I like cats.

Quality Reading Material

Want to give parents something really interesting to examine while they're waiting for their conference times? If so, then have each student make a personal riddle card. To make her riddle card, a student folds a sheet of white construction paper in half and writes a riddle that hints at her identity on the front of her card. Inside the card, she glues a picture of herself or a photocopy of her school picture and personalizes it. Then she decorates the entire card to reflect her interests, hobbies, and talents. Display the class collection of riddle cards in the hallway outside your door. While he is waiting for his turn, each parent can attempt to locate the riddle that describes his youngster.

Jolene Vereecke
Grandview Elementary School
Higginsville, MO

Say, "Cheese!"

If you're a bit of a shutterbug, put your school pictures on display so that parents can enjoy them while they're waiting to see you. Set a small cloth-covered table outside your classroom door. On the table, place a plant, perhaps some refreshments, and a photo album containing pictures of your students in action at school. When parents can see their children happily involved in school activities, it helps to get each conference off to a positive start.

Dee Borman, Pittsburgh, PA

Diane Afferton, Morrisville, PA

Student-Graded Report Card

Add new dynamics to your parent-teacher conferences by having each student complete a report card to assess his recent work. If desired, duplicate the report card on page 59, and have each student complete a copy. It's easy to scan the report card with parents during a conference and determine whether or not their child is aware of his strengths and weaknesses. This type of feedback from the student also gives some insight into his talents, motivation level, self-esteem, school-related problems, and feelings about school. With this input from the student, you and his parents can develop appropriate plans for assisting him.

Mary Koeck
Winneconne School
Winneconne, WI

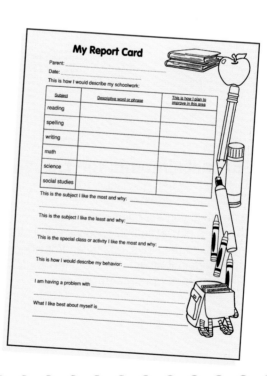

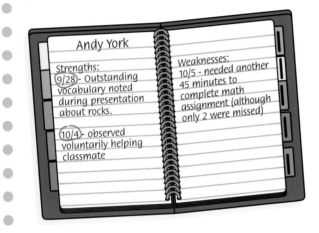

Keeping Notes

With a little preparation and periodical notations, a spiral notebook can become an invaluable conference tool. At even intervals, attach one personalized tab per student to a page in a spiral notebook. Use the pages behind each student's name to make dated notes regarding his strengths, weaknesses, and behaviors. Parents will appreciate the fact that you've been keeping detailed notes about their youngsters' progress. In addition, by viewing the notes with a parent, you may be able to piece together how outside events are affecting the student's schoolwork.

Vonda Davis
Bowling Green Primary
Caroline County, VA

Authentic Assessment

With the emphasis on portfolios and authentic assessment, you'll appreciate this suggestion that's high on student involvement. Prior to conference time, ask each student to select three pieces of his work that are his favorites. Then have him write (or dictate for you to write) on a separate Post-it note what it is about each of the work samples that he likes. Attach each note to the corresponding assignment. During conferences, parents will enjoy the notes as insights into their children's interests, concerns, and self-esteem levels.

Michele Lasky, Mandalay Elementary School, Wantagh, NY

Entertainment for the Younger Set

Since it's often necessary for parents to bring their young children to conferences, provide some things for youngsters to do while you are talking with their parents. In advance, arrange a play area and supply it with coloring books, crayons, games, toys, books, and/or videos. The children can entertain themselves during the conference, and you will experience fewer interruptions.

Sue Leahy
Rockford, IL

Check It Off

To help ensure that students arrive on the day of the field trip with the items they need, send home a pretrip checklist. Indicate which items are necessary and which ones are optional. Your students' parents will appreciate your forethought, and you'll be one step closer to a successful field trip.

Julie Eick Granchelli
Towne Elementary
Lockport, NY

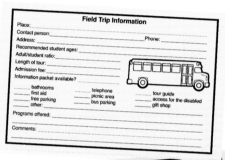

Color-Coded Nametags

Assign a color to each chaperone; then provide the chaperone and each student in his group with nametags of the same color. Chaperones and students can easily identify their groups. As an extra precaution, stamp the backs of all tags with a stamp bearing your school's return address.

Lining Up Chaperones

Lining up field trip chaperones is a perfect task for a parent volunteer. Provide the volunteer with the phone numbers of parents who have expressed an interest, the date and time of the upcoming field trip, a brief outline of what each chaperone is expected to do, and the number of chaperones needed. The parents will enjoy talking with one another, and you'll be free to attend to other field trip preparations.

Melissa Goldenberg
Oak Hill Elementary
Overland Park, KS

Field Trip Info

Organize important field trip information using the handy form on page 60. The form is a great planning tool, and after the trip it can be filed and used for future reference.

Field Trip Predictions

Museum Field Trip
We'll see
   mummies
   rocks
   bones
   paintings

Pretrip Predictions

Before leaving on a field trip, ask students to predict what they will see and learn on the trip. List all predictions on a large chart, and discuss why these predictions might come true. When you return, compare the actual events of the day to the list of predictions. If a prediction did not occur, have students suggest possible reasons.

A Class Plan

Lengthen the learning experience of your field trip by involving students in its planning stages. Enlist your students' help in brainstorming steps to organize the trip, a list of needed supplies, and so on. Troubleshooting the trip is also an invaluable lesson. To do this, ask students to anticipate problems that might occur during the trip and offer solutions to these problems. In the end, you'll have a well-planned trip and a group of youngsters who are committed to making it a successful experience for everyone involved.

Amy Kallelis—Gr. 3, Sanders Elementary, Smyrna, GA

Sparking Interest

To build student enthusiasm and knowledge about an upcoming field trip, prepare a pretrip scavenger hunt. Program a blank tic-tac-toe grid with eight different trip-related activities and one open space. Give each child a copy of the grid and ask her to write in her own idea in the open space. Instruct each student to draw an X over every activity she completes and an O over each one she chooses not to complete. To reward students for their pretrip investigations, attach a gold star to the field trip nametag of each child who earns three Xs in a row. Outstanding!

Debbie Erickson—Grs. 2–3 Multi-Age
Waterloo Elementary School
Waterloo, WI

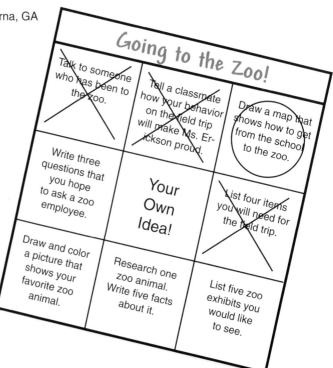

Going to the Zoo!

Talk to someone who has been to the zoo.	Tell a classmate how your behavior on the field trip will make Ms. Erickson proud.	Draw a map that shows how to get from the school to the zoo.
Write three questions that you hope to ask a zoo employee.	Your Own Idea!	List four items you will need for the field trip.
Draw and color a picture that shows your favorite zoo animal.	Research one zoo animal. Write five facts about it.	List five zoo exhibits you would like to see.

Classy Clipboards

If you require written work to be completed during a field trip, these easy-to-make clipboards are a must! From sturdy cardboard boxes, cut a 9" x 12" rectangle for each student and/or chaperone. Cover each rectangle with colorful Con-Tact covering and attach a medium-size binder clip to the top as shown. The binder clip holds paper and a pencil too! You can count on youngsters feeling quite important as they carry these classy clipboards with them throughout the trip.

Glorianne Bradshaw
Valley Elementary School
Crystal, ND

Top-Notch Behavior

Encourage students to be on their best behavior with this positive approach. Before departure, read aloud a list of expected field trip behaviors; then give each leader a copy of the list and a pencil. Ask each leader to note on her list the positive behaviors that she acknowledges and observes, as well as positive comments directed toward her group by another adult. Periodically check in with each leader to applaud her group's behavior. This positive outlook is sure to deliver top-notch results.

Susan K. Brighton—Gr. 3, Superior Elementary School, Superior, CO

Field Trip Books

These individual booklets are the perfect place for students to record their field trip observations. To make a book, stack several pieces of paper, fold the paper in half, and punch two holes near the folded edge. Next, thread a three- to four-foot length of yarn through both holes and securely tie the yarn ends. On the day of the trip, ask each child to personalize the front cover of a field trip book before she suspends the book from her neck. Provide each chaperone with pencils for her group members. At different points throughout the field trip, ask the chaperones to distribute the pencils so students can record their observations in their field trip books. When the observations are recorded and the pencils collected, proceed with the field trip. Each student will have a unique collection of notes by the time she returns to the classroom.

Karen Smith
Pine Lane Elementary Homeschool
Pace, FL

Field Trips

Chaperone Guidebooks

Individual guidebooks are a great way to ease the field trip jitters your chaperones might be experiencing. Compile a booklet of information for each chaperone that includes the name of each adult and the students in his or her group, a schedule for the day, a map of the field trip destination, a checklist of sights students should see, and guidelines for student behavior. The chances that your chaperones will remain cool, calm, and collected have just been tripled!

Kelly A. Lu—Gr. 2
Berlyn School
Ontario, CA

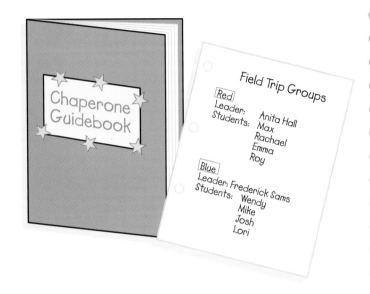

Busy on the Bus

If a lengthy bus ride is required to reach your destination, try this. Prior to boarding the bus, give each child a list of sights that can be seen along the bus route. Younger students can check off each one as they see it. Challenge older students to sequentially number the sights in the order they see them. Students will be so busy watching for upcoming landmarks that the time spent on the bus will fly by!

Julie Eick Granchelli, Towne Elementary, Lockport, NY

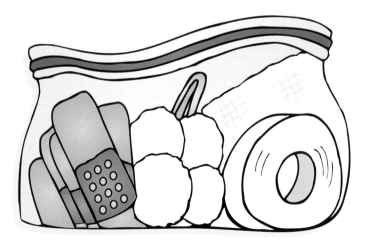

First Aid Kit

Be prepared for the unexpected! Pack a resealable plastic bag with a variety of first aid supplies, such as bandages, cotton balls, antibacterial cream, tweezers, gauze, and adhesive tape. Tuck the resulting kit in a tote bag or backpack that you plan to carry. In the event of a minor injury, you'll have just what you need right at hand.

Kimberly D. Nunes-Bufford—Grs. K–2
Jeter Primary
Opelika, AL

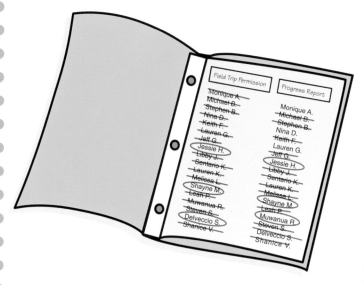

Paper Trail Notebook

Here's a simple system for tracking assorted parent correspondence, from field trip permission forms to conference slips to requests for supplies. Prepare a class list (or two), leaving blank space at the top of each list for a title. Keep a supply of the lists in a notebook at your desk. To track returned correspondence, appropriately title a class list and then mark out each child's name as you receive her paperwork. Circle the name of any student who forgets her paperwork and follow up with her. If your record keeping reveals that select students routinely need reminders, address the issue with the youngsters and their parents.

Nancy Long
Washington-Wilkes Primary School
Washington, GA

Planning Multiple Trips

If you are fortunate enough to take your class on several field trips, here's a tip for you. In a small, inexpensive address book, log the name and address of each field trip contact person with whom you work. The resulting resource will be invaluable as you plan future trips. In fact, you may wish to call each contact person before you close out your classroom for summer break. Booking trips this far in advance will help you secure dates and times that perfectly match your curriculum needs.

Christine A. Bates—Gr. 3, Arlington Christian Academy, Akron, OH

Nifty Nametags

These easy-to-make clip-on nametags are versatile and durable! For each nametag you will need a plastic clip clothespin (with a hole in the handle) and a brass fastener. Personalize and laminate a poster board nametag for each youngster. Then punch a hole in the top of each nametag. Using brass fasteners, attach each nametag to a clothespin. To wear the nametags, students simply clip the clothespins to their clothing. It doesn't matter how the clothespin is clipped, since the nametag can rotate on the brass fastener.

Marlene Klukken
Blue Grass Elementary School
Knoxville, TN

Seasonal Incentive

The holiday season challenges even the best classroom management skills. To make an incentive display, trace the outline of a holiday design onto poster board. Cut the design into puzzle pieces. Position and trace the pieces onto the poster board outline. Reward good classroom behaviors by attaching puzzle pieces to the outline. When the puzzle is complete, reward each student with a small candy cane.

Susan Valenti
Emmitsburg, MD

Classroom Party Management

To prevent classroom parties from getting out of hand, you might try this behavior-modification technique: Draw five vertical lines on the board before the party begins. Explain that rowdy behavior will result in a line being erased. If all lines are erased, the party is over.

Debbie Retzlaff—Gr. 3, Van Voorhis Elementary School, Fort Knox, KY

Party Donations

Request donations for classroom party refreshments using the form on page 61. On a copy of the form, list desired refreshments and supplies; then sign your name. Send home a copy with each child. File the returned response slips for easy reference.

Linnae Granger-Nicholas
Cuba, NY

Homework Helpers

Establish this homework routine to promote parental involvement. Attach a self-sticking dot to each homework paper. When a student's homework is completed, have him ask his parent to check it. After any necessary corrections have been made by the student, the parent draws a smiley face atop the sticky dot. Now homework will return completed, checked, and corrected!

Sheila R. Chapman
Atkinson School
Newnan, GA

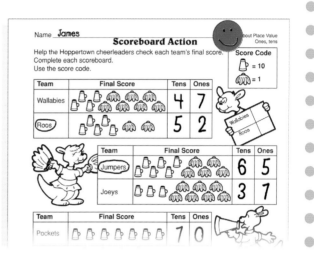

Team Spirit

When students have trouble getting all of their assignments in on time, work on team spirit. Divide the class into teams of three to four students. Draw a class football field on the blackboard. Each time every member of the team brings in an assignment, let the team move its football five yards down the field. Reward the team that scores the first touchdown.

Linda Reeves, Orchard Avenue School, Grand Junction, CO

Plastic Eggs

To encourage completion of homework and following class rules, give every student a plastic egg with a number in it each morning. Students keep the eggs at their desks unless they have to return them to the basket on the teacher's desk. A student must return his egg if his homework is not completed or if he breaks a class rule. At the end of the day, the teacher draws a number to select the student who receives a treat.

Debbie Retzlaff—Gr. 3

Homework

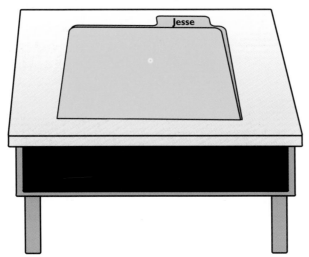

Homework Folders

Save time collecting homework each morning with homework folders. Label and laminate a folder for each child. Each morning, place the folders atop your youngsters' desks. When a student arrives, he slips his homework assignment(s) in his folder and places the folder in a designated tray. One quick look at the remaining folders identifies students who have not turned in their homework. Reward each student who turns in satisfactory work by attaching a sticker to his folder.

Phyllis Handler—Gr. 2
Arnold Elementary,
Dover, DE

Homework Alert!

Do your students lose their homework assignments in the shuffle of papers that go home daily? Then try this helpful reminder. Keep a small strip of paper labeled "Homework—Please Return" near your duplicating materials. Before duplicating a homework assignment, place the labeled strip at the top of the paper. Parents will be alerted to these assignments, ensuring more prompt returns.

Rosemary Kavner—Gr. 2, Elizabeth Lenz School, Reno, NV

Paper Carriers

Papers will arrive home safely when students use these sturdy paper carriers. Remove the lid from a clean, empty Pringle's potato crisps can before covering it with Con-Tact paper. Use a permanent marker to label each can with a child's name. Punch two holes on each side of the can as shown, tie each end of a ribbon or yarn length through one pair of holes, and replace the lid. Throughout the day, have each student place his graded papers or important messages in his paper carrier. Students take their paper carriers home each afternoon and return them the following morning.

Marilyn Borden—Gr. 3
Castleton Elementary School
Bomoseen, VT

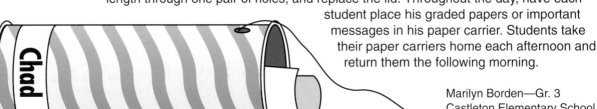

Student Checklists

A supply of student checklists can save you time in a variety of ways! Use a checklist to determine which students have not turned in a homework assignment or still need to return a permission form. Keep track of parent communications on a student checklist, or monitor which students have received positive notes from you during the month. You can also place a checklist at a center and ask students to cross off their names as they complete the center activity. The possibilities are endless!

Susan Sawyer—Gr. 2
Hickory Elementary
Bel Air, MD

Homework Clip Chart

Keeping track of homework assignments is easy with this handy system. In a prominent area display a chart labeled with each child's name. Near the chart, place a basket of clothespins. When a child has a homework assignment, he clips a clothespin next to his name. When he returns the assignment, he removes the clothespin from the chart. This system enables you to see at a glance which students have returned their homework assignments.

Marci Godfrey—Gr. 2, South Knoll Elementary, Bryan, TX

Homework Houses

A student's homework is less likely to become lost at home when it's safe inside a homework house. To make a homework house, have each student decorate and personalize a shoebox. Before the youngsters take their projects home, tuck a contract (similar to the one shown) inside each house. Challenge each youngster to find a strategic location for his homework house, such as the first place he sees upon arriving home and the last place he sees as he departs for school each morning. Also instruct him to complete his homework contract with the help of a parent. Remind him to place the completed contract in his homework house so that he will remember to return it to school the next day.

Students can quickly establish the routine of depositing their homework assignments in their homework houses as soon as they arrive home. Later, when it's time to complete their homework, the students know where the homework can be found. Encourage parents to check the homework houses each evening to verify that their youngsters' assignments are ready to be returned to school.

Terrific Tickets

This idea is just the ticket for motivating students to complete their homework on time! Each morning give a raffle ticket to every student who completes her homework assignment. A student writes her name on the back of her ticket and drops it in a designated container. On Friday draw several tickets from the container, and award each selected student a special treat or privilege. Then discard the personalized tickets and repeat the procedure the following week.

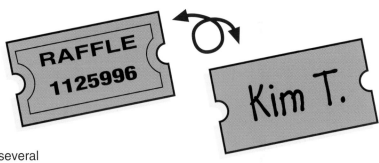

Benita Kuhlman
Avon Elementary
Avon, SD

Homework Incentive

This suspenseful reward system makes children excited to turn in their homework assignments. Each day record the names of children who bring in their homework assignments. At the end of each week, place slips of paper labeled with the days of the week into a box; then choose one slip of paper from the box. Students who turned in their homework on the chosen day receive prizes. The prizewinning homework day is always a surprise, so students are eager to turn in their assignments each day.

Jo Ann White—Gr. 2, Decker School, Mt. Arlington, NJ

 Homework

Reading:

Math:

Spelling: Study your words!
Test on Friday.

Science: Check your mold experiment. Write an observation in your journal.

Social Studies:

Other:

Colorful Homework Chart

Help students keep homework assignments organized with a color-coded homework chart. To create the chart, title a piece of chart paper "Homework"; then write each subject heading in its own color. Laminate and display the resulting chart. When you give a homework assignment, use the appropriate color of wipe-off marker to write the assignment beside its corresponding subject area. After an assignment is collected, wipe the related programming from the chart.

Krista Paciello—Gr. 3
St. Catherine-Labouré School
Wheaton, MD

Dear __Mom and Dad__ ,

Dec. 9, 2004
Date

I forgot to turn in my homework today. My assignment was __to put my spelling words in ABC order__ .

Please sign and date this form. I must return it with my completed homework assignment on __Wednesday, Dec. 10, 2004__ .
day of the week   date

Parent Signature

Date

Love,
Patrick
Student Signature

Oops! Notice

How often have you heard the phrase "Oops! I forgot!" when collecting homework assignments? These reminder notices are an effective way to foster responsibility in your students. Make a supply of the notices on page 62. Each time a student forgets to turn in a homework assignment, have him complete and carry home a notice that must be returned with a parent signature the following school day. With this homework plan in place, forgotten homework could soon be obsolete!

Patricia Dent—Gr. 3
Kindle School
Pitman, NJ

Take a Number, Please

Make the time students must wait for you to check their work more productive with this numerical system. Number seasonal cutouts to correspond to your enrollment. Stack the cutouts numerically. When a student completes his work, he takes the top cutout from the stack. He then returns to his seat and reads a library book until his number is called. "Number 15, please."

Mary Hess—Gr. 3. Naples, FL

Homework Help

Taking a weekly approach to homework assignments benefits students and you! On Monday send home a copy of page 63 that lists the homework assignments for the week. Then, on Friday, collect the students' homework along with their parent-signed assignment sheets. Students (and their parents) appreciate the flexibility of this approach, and you'll find that you spend less time checking homework. In addition, you have a ready-to-file record of each child's weekly homework efforts.

Angela Story—Gr. 2
Cedar Road Elementary
Chesapeake, VA

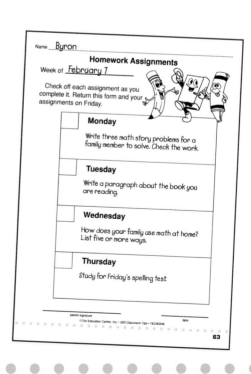

Name __Byron__

Homework Assignments

Week of __February 7__

Check off each assignment as you complete it. Return this form and your assignments on Friday.

Monday
Write three math story problems for a family member to solve. Check the work.

Tuesday
Write a paragraph about the book you are reading.

Wednesday
How does your family use math at home? List five or more ways.

Thursday
Study for Friday's spelling test.

parent signature   date

©The Education Center, Inc. • 500 Classroom Tips • TEC60848

63

Personalized Clothespins

Personalized clothespins keep each student's work together, helping to identify nameless papers. Program a wooden clothespin with each child's name before having him decorate it. Clip the decorated clothespins to a wire basket. When a child finishes all of his seatwork, he clips it together with his personalized clothespin and deposits it in the basket. A glance at the clothespins remaining on the basket will indicate students who are still completing seatwork.

Peggy English
Lexington Elementary
Lexington, OK

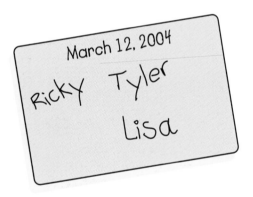

Homework Tracker

Add a collection officer to your job chart, and you'll find it's a breeze to keep up with homework assignments. At the start of each day, have your collection officer gather the previous day's homework assignment. If a student neglected to do his homework, the collection officer has the student sign a dated card. You can quickly examine the card to see whose homework is missing. These dated cards are also easy to store for future reference, such as during conference and report card times.

Shannon Reinighaus—Gr. 2
Lowry Elementary
Tampa, FL

Handy Homework Collection

Spend less time checking for homework with this clever collection idea! Suspend a length of clothesline across a bulletin board or an unused section of the chalkboard. Personalize a clothespin for each student. Clip the clothespins to the line in alphabetical order at about three-inch intervals. A part of each student's morning routine is to clip his homework to the clothesline. When you remove the papers, you'll know in an instant if any homework is missing.

Kathleen Radtke—Gr. 2
Crocker Elementary
Crocker, MO

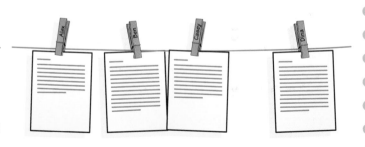

Weekly Assignment Sheets

Students and parents with busy after-school schedules will appreciate being notified of each week's homework assignments on Monday afternoons. Duplicate the weekly list on bright neon paper so it is easy to identify. The list can also serve as a reminder of special school activities that have been planned for the week. Ask that each student return his list, with his homework assignments attached, by Friday. Because of the flexibility of this system, it will undoubtedly be well received by both your students and their parents.

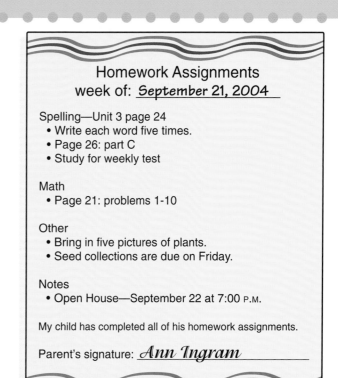

Homework Assignments week of: _September 21, 2004_

Spelling—Unit 3 page 24
• Write each word five times.
• Page 26: part C
• Study for weekly test

Math
• Page 21: problems 1-10

Other
• Bring in five pictures of plants.
• Seed collections are due on Friday.

Notes
• Open House—September 22 at 7:00 P.M.

My child has completed all of his homework assignments.

Parent's signature: _Ann Ingram_

A Monthly Hoedown

The anticipation of a party at the end of the month can keep your youngsters on track with their homework responsibilities. Using individual incentive charts (page 64) or monthly calendars, keep track of each youngster's daily homework assignments. At the end of the month, invite all students who successfully completed their assignments for the entire month to a special homework party. Each month, ask parent volunteers to prepare and serve a different treat such as ice cream, trail mix, or fruit kabobs. What a yummy way to celebrate!

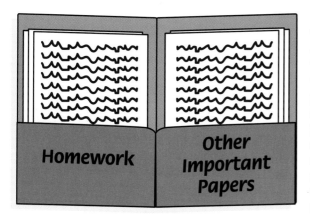

Homework   **Other Important Papers**

Folders to Go

Personalized homework folders help ensure that homework and other important papers reach home safely. Personalize a two-pocket folder for each student. Label one pocket "Homework" and one pocket "Other Important Papers." Near the end of each day, have students tuck their homework papers and any other important notes and/or memos in the appropriate pockets of their homework folders. Request that parents check the contents of their children's folders each day. Also encourage parents to review their youngsters' completed homework and assure that the assignments are returned in the folders the following day. These handy folders will quickly become a regular part of your students' daily routines, and they won't leave home without them!

Homework

Individual Incentives

Using this incentive plan, students chart their own homework progress. Have each student personalize a construction paper copy of the incentive chart on page 64. Each time a student satisfactorily completes and returns a homework assignment, present him with a sticker for his chart. When all of the squares on his chart contain stickers, allow the student to select a prize from a classroom prize box or to choose a special privilege.

An All-Star Plan

Motivate students to complete and return their homework assignments on time with this star-studded plan. Cut five large star shapes from yellow poster board. Laminate the cutouts for durability; then attach a strip of magnetic tape to the back of each cutout. Each day that all of your students complete and return their homework assignments, attach one cutout to the chalkboard (or another magnetic surface). When all five stars are posted, reward your students with five minutes of extra recess or another special privilege.

And the Winner Is...

Encourage better homework habits with this game of chance. On a sheet of poster board, design, program, and laminate a grid similar to the one shown. When a student completes and returns a homework assignment on time, he writes his name (using a wipe-off marker) in an empty square on the grid. When all of the squares are filled, hold a lottery drawing. To do this, program a set of two-inch construction paper squares with the numerals 1–8. Program a second set of squares (of a different color) with the letters in the word *homework*. Combine the squares in a Ziploc bag; then remove one square of each color. Call out the winning coordinates and reward the student whose name is written in the corresponding square with a free homework coupon (page 65). And the winner is...H3!

☺	H	O	M	E	W	O	R	K
1	Adam							
2							Josh	
3		Katie						
4				Seth				
5								
6							Kelly	
7								
8			Ali			Kyle		

Line Monitor

Your students will line up more quickly and quietly under the watchful eye of a line leader who doubles as a monitor. Only when everyone is quiet and standing in a straight line will the monitor lead the class to its destination. This helper also has the option of stopping the line whenever she hears talking. When your line leader is at work, you can just stand back and watch.

Barbara McCool—Gr. 3
North Jackson Elementary School
Brandon, MS

Shhhh.

Waiting for Special Secrets

Whenever students must wait in line for several minutes, quiet the line by sharing a special secret with each child. Beginning with the quietest child, whisper a personalized, positive message to each of your students. Students will learn to wait more quietly anticipating these special secrets.

Kimberlee Whatley, Bridgeton Christian School, Bridgeton, NJ

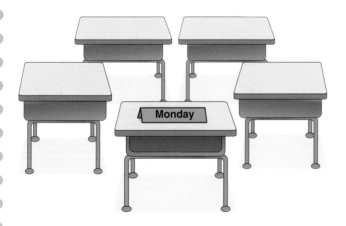

Monday

Daily Lineup

Keep students lining up in an orderly fashion day after day! Arrange the students' desks in five groups and name each group for a different weekday. A group lines up first during its namesake day. The first group is followed in line by the group named for the next weekday, and then the next, and so on until all groups are in line. With this systematic approach, lining up quickly and quietly soon becomes a habit!

Pat Hart—Gr. 2
C. A. Henning School
Troy, IL

Cut Passes

Use this idea to minimize problems when students are lining up to leave the room. At the beginning of the year, give each child a cut pass like the one shown. If a child wants to cut in line so that he can stand near a friend, he forfeits his pass to the person he cut in front of. Since children rarely want to give up their cut passes, this idea works like a charm.

Mardi Dilks—Gr. 3
Cooper City Elementary
Cooper City, FL

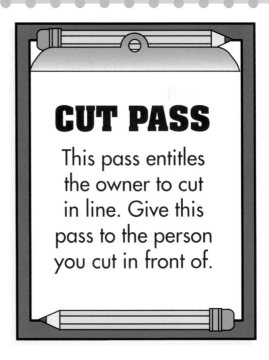

CUT PASS

This pass entitles the owner to cut in line. Give this pass to the person you cut in front of.

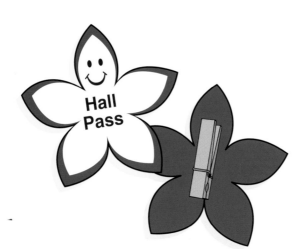

Hall Pass

Missing Hall Passes

If your hall passes seem to suddenly disappear, try this! Glue a clip-on clothespin to the back of each pass. Then have students clip the passes to their clothing before leaving the room. No more missing passes!

Sue Hancock
Seaford Christian Academy
Seaford, DE

Right on Time

How many times have you forgotten to ready a student for early pickup? Try this! Place a manipulative clock on the student's desk; then, with the student's help, program it to show a time that is five minutes before his parent is scheduled to arrive. When the times on the class clock and the manipulative clock match, the youngster clears his desk and gathers his things. His actions will prompt you to take care of other necessary preparations, and by the time his parent arrives, the child will be ready to go!

Rita Yanoff—Gr. 2
Sussex Christian School
Hope, NJ

Hallway Manners

Here's an upbeat way to quickly settle your troop before leading it into the hallway. When the class is lined up, sing each line of the cadence call shown, pausing for students to repeat each line after you. This military-style chant readies your brigade to march through the hall with pride!

Amy Kallelis
Cold Spring Elementary
Doylestown, PA

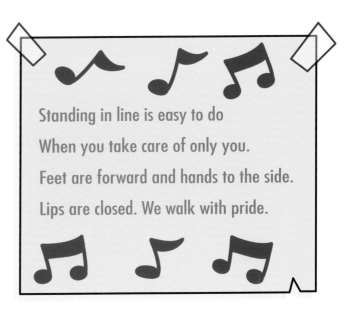

Standing in line is easy to do

When you take care of only you.

Feet are forward and hands to the side.

Lips are closed. We walk with pride.

Fire Drill Reminder

I converted a bulletin board figure (page 66) into a fire drill aid which is especially helpful for substitute teachers. I post the fire drill route on the cutout, along with a press-on pocket. I place a class roster in the pocket before mounting the cutout near the exit. As I (or the substitute) leave the room, I grab the roster so that I can check to insure everyone is in line.

Marilyn Borden—Gr. 3
Castleton Elementary School
Bomoseen, VT

Lunch Count

A Lunch-Count Graph

Morning Lunch Count

Here's a quick and easy way to practice estimation skills. Use a permanent felt-tip marker to label a sand pail "Lunch Pail." If desired cut pictures of food items from magazines and attach the pictures to the pail. Put a supply of yellow and brown Unifix cubes next to the pail. Each morning when a student arrives at school, he puts a brown cube in the pail if he has brought his lunch from home. If he is purchasing his lunch from the school cafeteria, he puts a yellow cube in the pail. After each child has had a turn, have students peek in the pail and estimate how many of each color cube are there. Then empty the pail and have students help you count the number of yellow and brown cubes. Use the gathered information to ask students math-related questions and to create a lunch-count bar graph.

Alison Whitney—Gr. 2
Miramar Elementary
Miramar, FL

Money Holders

Recycle 35mm film containers as student money holders. Ask parents to collect the containers, or check film-processing stores. Label each container with a child's name and teacher's name for easy return if misplaced. Have each child carry his money to and from school in his container.

Retha Mancil
Fort Rucker Elementary School
Ozark, AL

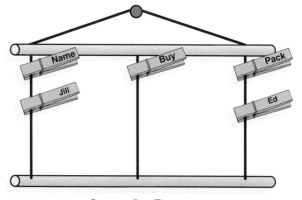

Lunch Count
and Attendance Taker

To avoid early-morning chaos in your class-room, use this quick lunch "counter." Assemble the hanger as illustrated using two dowel rods and four twelve-inch pieces of clothesline. Write each student's name on a clothespin. As students enter the classroom, they pin their clothespins under "Buy" or "Pack." The remaining pins are absentees.

Idea by:
Dr. Carl Callenback, Elizabethtown, PA

Adapted by:
Diane Jameson, Downingtown, PA

Sign In, Please

Instantly put your youngsters' writing and thinking skills into gear with this morning routine. Attach a supply of charts, such as the one shown, to each of several clipboards. (You will need one clipboard per row, group, or table.) Before the youngsters arrive each morning, place each group's clipboard in a designated location. The first child in each group to arrive writes his name, his lunch plans, and his after-school plans on the chart. He passes the chart to another student in his group. The completed charts are then passed to the teacher who calculates the daily lunch and attendance counts. The task of writing the daily information on a chart helps reinforces a student's thinking process, and it provides the teacher with valuable information.

Diane Bodnar
Jefferson Elementary
Bettendorf, IA

Name	Hot or Cold Lunch	After-School Plans
Deon	hot	go to scouts
Maria	hot	ride bus home

Lunch-Count Savvy

Put math on the menu with a daily problem-solving activity! Each morning have a different child tally the classroom lunch chart to determine how many children are ordering hot lunch. Then invite the rest of the class to guess the total number of hot-lunch orders. The child in charge responds to each guess by stating whether the guess is greater than or less than the hot-lunch order. For a greater challenge, ask students to present each guess in a number sentence like "Six plus two equals eight hot-lunch orders for today." Students will surely eat up this daily math warm-up!

Jan Smith, Foothill Elementary, Boulder, CO

Open House

Welcome Mats

When parents see these student-made greetings, they'll smile from ear to ear! To make a desktop welcome mat, a student embellishes a 12" x 18" sheet of construction paper with a welcome message and other desired decorations. On the day of open house, have each child tape his mat atop his desk as he leaves school for the day. As parents arrive, point out the personalized greetings their children have prepared for them and suggest that they write their children personal notes of thanks and encouragement. These notes may be written either on the mats or on provided notepaper. When students find the notes the following day, it will be their turn to smile from ear to ear!

Sally Dederich
Peshtigo Elementary School
Peshtigo, WI

Conference Requested

Use the conference request form on page 67 to show your enthusiasm for keeping the lines of parent-teacher communication open. Duplicate and cut apart a supply of the forms; then distribute approximately five forms to each family. (Later send forms home to the parents who were unable to attend open house.) Encourage parents to complete and submit requests whenever they feel there are concerns that need to be discussed. Parents will appreciate the ease with which they can set up special conferences and your willingness to meet with them.

Chinita Hodo—Gr. 2, Redan Elementary School, Redan, GA

OPEN HOUSE VISITORS

Students	□	□	□	□	□	□							
Moms	□	□	□	□	□								
Dads	□	□	□	□	□	□	□	□					
Sisters	□	□	□										
Brothers	□	□											
Grandparents	□	□	□										
Friends	□	□	□										

Open House Graph

Here's a nifty way to turn your open house participation into a high-interest graphing activity. On a length of bulletin board paper, design a graph like the one shown above. As visitors enter your room on open house night, ask them to write their names on individual sticky notes and attach their personalized notes to the graph. The next day have students use the graph to answer questions about open house attendance.

Lora McGinn
Strawberry Park Elementary
Steamboat Springs, CO

Picture This!

This photo display gives parents a clear picture of what their children do during a typical day. Write a student-generated list of school day activities that includes all subject areas, special classes, lunch and recesses. Assign one activity from the list to each child; then over the course of the next few days, photograph each child participating in his assigned activity. Also ask each child to write a paragraph that describes his assigned activity for this project. Mount each snapshot and its corresponding paragraph on a 9" x 12" sheet of construction paper. Sequence the projects so that they portray a typical school day and mount them on a large display area (such as a hallway wall) with the caption "Picture This! Learning Is Fun!"

Lisa Fritz, Hawthorne Elementary School, Indianapolis, IN

Scheduling Conferences

Scheduling parent-teacher conferences is an enormous task. To lighten the load of this responsibility, give your open house guests the opportunity to sign up for their conferences in advance. On open house night display a sign-up sheet—complete with dates and times—for parent-teacher conferences. Ask each parent to sign up for the time that best fits his or her schedule. As conference time draws near, schedule those parents who were unable to attend open house; then notify all families of their scheduled conference times. Involving your entire school in this scheduling system allows parents with more than one child to coordinate their conference times with ease.

Principal and Staff, Westside Elementary, Stoughton, WI

Just for Our Guests!

These kid-created activities may be just the ticket to boost your open house attendance. A few days before open house, ask each of several small groups to plan an estimation activity for the upcoming event. Activities might include estimating the number of items in a jar; estimating the circumference of a pumpkin, watermelon, or other large fruit; or guessing the weight of a small object. Over the next few days, with your students' assistance, set up the activities around the classroom. Once the activities are in place, ask each group to find the answer to its estimating challenge and design an award to present to the guest who submits the most accurate estimate. Inform your students' parents of the activities in an open House invitation. Also indicate the time at which the winners will be recognized. Make arrangements for two or more members from each group to be present open house night so that these students can determine the winners of the activities and present the awards. And the winner of the pumpkin activity is...!

Guess the circumference of the pumpkin in inches.

Place your guess in the box.

Mary Jo Kampschnieder—Gr. 2
Howells Community Catholic School
Howells, NE

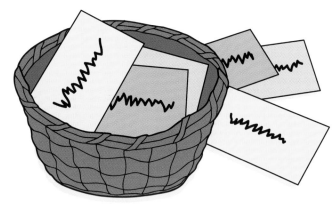

Voluntary Contributions

Encourage classroom contributions without a lot of fanfare. During your open house presentation, show your guests a basketful of colorful index cards. Explain that the cards are labeled with inexpensive items (such as paper plates, pipe cleaners, cassette tapes, and grading stickers) that will be used during the school year. Place the basket near the door and invite parents who are interested in making classroom contributions to choose cards before they leave. Each time a donation is received, send a personal note of thanks to the appropriate family.

Leigh Anne Newsom—Gr. 3
Greenbrier Intermediate
Chesapeake, VA

Puzzles to Solve

Here's a neat way to encourage parents to interact during open house. On each of three or four tables, display the pieces of a different classroom jigsaw puzzle. Before your guests arrive, take several pieces from each display and place them in a basket. As you greet your guests at the door, hand each one a puzzle piece from the basket. The guest determines which jigsaw puzzle his piece belongs to, then works to complete the puzzle with the other parents who received similar puzzle pieces. As you mingle among the tables, encourage conversation between the parents. After several minutes proceed with your planned presentation. In addition to being an excellent icebreaker, this activity promotes friendships among parents.

Jeannette Freeman, Baldwin School of Puerto Rico, Guaynabo, Puerto Rico

Survival Kits

Homework survival kits make tackling homework a cinch! To make a starter kit for each student, tuck two pencils, an eraser, and a ruler in a small gift bag or box. On the evening of open house, set the starter kits atop your students' desks and ask parents to take the kits home to their children. Encourage parents to add a few more supplies to the kits, such as crayons, scissors, and glue—emphasizing the convenience of having these supplies on hand. Also explain that the kits can increase the appeal of homework assignments when the supplies are used only for homework purposes. To encourage your students to continue using their homework survival kits, surprise them with gifts for their kits on holidays and/or special occasions.

Top-of-the-Line Tour Guides

Make Open House a positive experience for you, your students, and their parents. Ask students to brainstorm open house attractions located in your classroom and around the school, and list their ideas on the chalkboard. Then ask each student to choose five items from the list and write them on a duplicated tour plan like the one shown. (Note that mandatory tour stops are already listed.) On the afternoon of open house, give each student his personalized open house itinerary. As an added incentive, promise stickers to students who attend open house and guide their guests through their tours. If a youngster and his parent(s) are unable to attend open house, suggest that the student ask his parent(s) to sign his tour plan after he has described each stop on the tour. Then award a sticker to each youngster who returns a signed tour plan.

Julie Renkes—Gr. 3, Dassel Elementary, Dassel, MN

Open House Tour

Please make each of the tour stops listed below with your child. The top five points of interest were selected by your child. We hope you enjoy your visit!

1.
2.
3.
4.
5.
6. Say hello to Mrs. Renkes.
7. Check out the sign-up sheets on the back table.
8. Sign up for a conference time in the small gym.

I completed the tour with my child.

_____
(signature)

Pop Quiz!

Students will enjoy turning the tables on their parents with this open house activity! With your youngsters' help, brainstorm a list of questions that could determine how well parents know their children. Questions might include "What is the name of your child's favorite book?", "What is your child's favorite food?", and "What does your child like to do in his or her spare time?" Use the list of questions to create a pop quiz for your open house visitors. On the evening of open house place copies of the quiz on your students' desks. Encourage all visiting parents to complete the quiz. Students will have a blast grading these papers!

Bonnie Coddington—Gr. 2, Voorhees School, South Bound Brook, NJ

Input From Parents

Invite your guests to share written comments about their open house visit using the questionnaire on page 68. For visibility, duplicate the questionnaire on neon-colored paper; then present one to each youngster's parent(s). This particular questionnaire encourages parents to describe the positive experiences they shared with their youngsters during open house. The resulting information helps reveal parents' perceptions of their children. In addition, the questionnaire provides an opportunity for parents to express any concerns they have.

Joann DeRosa, Samuel Smith School, Riverton, NJ

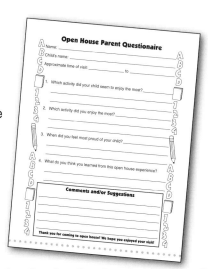

Pencil Sharpener Solution

Here's an easy way to avoid interruptions caused by students sharpening their pencils. Place a container of sharpened pencils and a sign-out sheet near the class sharpener. If a student suddenly finds herself needing to sharpen her pencil at an inappropriate time, she signs one out. Later, during an approved time, she sharpens her pencil and she sharpens and returns the one she borrowed. No more interruptions!

Kim Noviello—Gr. 3
JFK Primary Center
New Castle, PA

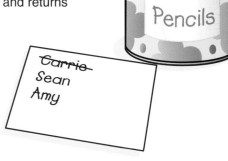

Pencil Sharpener Cover-Up

Here's an easy way to signal when students may sharpen their pencils. When you don't want students using the pencil sharpener, simply slip an empty, cube-shaped, decorative tissue box over it. Remove the decorative box to signal that pencils may be sharpened. Now that's a sharp idea!

Nancy Y. Karpyk—Gr. 2
Broadview Elementary
Weirton, WV

Pencil Passes

Minimize unnecessary pencil sharpening with this tip! Make a copy of the pencil patterns on page 69, program the pencils as shown, and make a class supply. At the begining of each week, issue each student a desired number of pencil-sharpening passes. Before sharpening his pencil, a student must deposit one pass in a designated container. Students will quickly learn to only sharpen their pencils when it is necessary.

Rebecca Gibson Calton
Auburn, AL

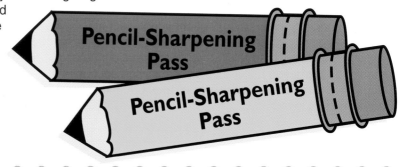

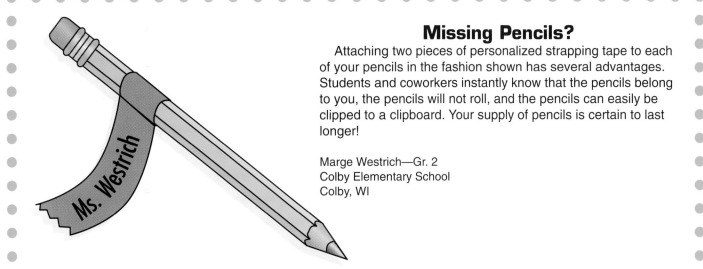

Missing Pencils?

Attaching two pieces of personalized strapping tape to each of your pencils in the fashion shown has several advantages. Students and coworkers instantly know that the pencils belong to you, the pencils will not roll, and the pencils can easily be clipped to a clipboard. Your supply of pencils is certain to last longer!

Marge Westrich—Gr. 2
Colby Elementary School
Colby, WI

The Borrow Box

If a student has lost or misplaced his pencil, where should he turn? To the borrow box! At the start of the school year, ask each student's family to donate a package of pencils. Sharpen several pencils and use a permanent marker to number each one. Store the numbered pencils in a decorated box and place a notepad nearby. If a student needs to borrow a pencil, he writes his name and the number of the pencil he is borrowing on the notepad. At the end of the day, ask the class helper to make sure that all borrowed pencils have been sharpened and returned. Now there's no need to spend valuable class time searching for missing pencils!

Jennifer Moody—Gr. 3, Winship Magnet School, Macon, GA

Hand-Raising Help

If you're constantly reminding students to raise their hands, try this! At the front of the classroom, display a large laminated grid that has 100 or more blank spaces. Each time students remember to raise their hands, use a wipe-off marker to color or check off one space on the grid. When the grid is full, present the class with a predetermined reward. Then wipe the grid clean and use it to reinforce another positive behavior!

Christy Reichard—Grs. 1–5 Special Education
Campbell Elementary School
Springfield, MO

Raise Your Hand!

Daily Schedule

Keep your youngsters abreast of each day's events by posting your daily schedule on a pocket chart. Write the numerals 1 through 12 on index cards; then position the cards in sequential order on the chart. Next, cut a supply of sentence strips in half and label each strip with the name of a different subject, class, or event that takes place on a recurring basis. To program the chart, position the labeled strips on the pocket chart in the order that they will occur. Store any unused strips nearby. At the end of each day, reprogram the chart to show the next day's schedule of events.

Tricia Peña—Gr. 3
Acacia Elementary
Vail, AZ

	Daily Schedule		
1	Opening	9	Lunch
2	Spelling	10	Math
3	Reading	11	Presentations
4	Group	12	Science
5	Art		
6	Recess		
7	Story		
8	P.E.		

Centers

Reports

Games

Special Classes

These hands-on reminders help individual students remember their special classes. Copy a supply of clock-face cards from page 70. Program one card for each special class that a youngster attends. (See sample card.) Next label and display a card pocket for each day of the week. Store the programmed cards in these pockets. Each morning distribute the cards for that day. A student keeps his card on his desk as a reminder. Then, after he returns from his special class, he replaces the card in its corresponding pocket.

Kim Schultze, Silver Spring, MD

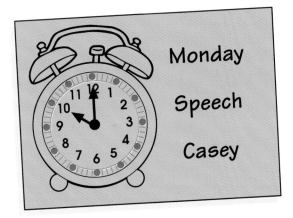

Monday

Speech

Casey

Specials of the Day

These handy reminders guard against forgetfulness! Label one poster board rectangle for each day of the school week. On each resulting poster, list the names and times of the specially scheduled classes your youngsters attend during that day. Keep all five posters on display at once, or put a class helper in charge of displaying the appropriate daily poster. Substitute teachers also find the posters especially helpful.

Sue Fichter—Gr. 2
St. Mary School
Des Plaines, IL

MONDAY'S SPECIALS

10:30-11:00	Music
1:00-1:40	Library
2:00-2:30	Computer Lab

Ron	Noel
Pete	Lester
Sarah	Jan

Transition Apron

Be prepared for students who complete assigned tasks by wearing a transition apron. Make or buy an apron. Sew on several pockets in different colors. Write tasks on index cards and place them in the pockets. After students complete classwork, they may either select an activity from a pocket on the apron or be assigned a card by the teacher.

Betty Ruth Baker
Director of Early Childhood Education
Baylor University
Waco, TX

Quick Transitions

Before students leave for lunch, recess, or special classes, ask them to place the books and materials needed for their next lesson atop their desks. Students are motivated to get ready quickly, and the succeeding lesson can begin immediately upon their return.

Geraldine Fulton—Gr. 3, Meadow Heights Elementary, Sedgewickville, MO

Beat the Clock

For those children having trouble organizing bookbags and desks first thing in the morning, play "Beat the Clock." The first week students have five minutes to get organized, the second four minutes, the third three minutes, and the fourth two minutes. Individual records are kept on index cards. Each day punch the cards of students who beat the clock. Awards are given on Friday. By the end of one month, my students are ready to start class on time.

Mary Anne Haffner—Gr. 3
Waynesboro, PA

David's Beat-the-Clock Card

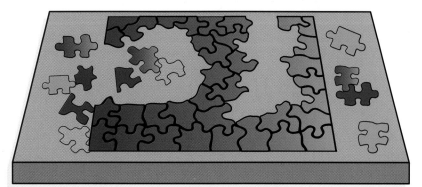

Puzzle Power

To reduce homeroom chaos, my students may work at an ongoing puzzle table as they arrive. On rainy days, we have a puzzle contest between groups of six to eight children. Each group is given a puzzle with the same number of pieces. The group to assemble its puzzle first wins a prize.

Sr. Margaret Ann
Emmitsburg, MD

Classical Classroom Management

I have found that playing classical music after high-energy activities such as P.E. and recess helps to calm my students. In addition, prepare a brief, transitional activity such as a handwriting assignment for the students to complete as soon as they return. Students' energies are quickly soothed and redirected with a minimal amount of effort.

Wiley W. Blevins, Frederick, MD

Mail Call!

Encourage written communication from students with this extra-time activity. Place a mailbox or a mailbox-type receptacle in a prominent classroom location. Label it with a fictitious address such as the one shown, and place a container of large, lined index cards nearby. When a student has extra time, he illustrates the blank side of a card to resemble a postcard. Then he divides the lined side of the card in half. On the left half, he writes a message to you. On the right half, he writes your name and the posted address, then illustrates a stamp. He places the card in the mailbox and, if necessary, raises the flag. At the end of the day, remove the mail and lower the flag. Acknowledge each child's correspondence with a verbal thank-you or, as time permits, with a written response.

Ms. Ohlson
16 Learning Lane
Teacher Town, VA

Debby Ohlson—Art Teacher
Fredericksburg Academy
Fredericksburg, VA

Free-Time Schedule

Looking for a way to eliminate the phrase "What do I do now?" from your students' vocabularies? Here's an idea for you. Design and laminate a free-time schedule that lists the days of the week. Then, using a wipe-off marker, program the schedule with five different free-time activities. Display the poster in a prominent classroom location. When a student completes an assignment, she looks at the schedule to determine the free-time activity for the day. Reprogram the schedule each week to add variety!

Mary Jo Kampschnieder—Gr. 2
Howells Community Catholic School
Howells, NE

Free-Time Schedule

Monday: Read a book.

Tuesday: Write in your journal.

Wednesday: Play a learning game.

Thursday: Make a card for a friend.

Friday: Free choice!

Day by Day

If free-time choices in your classroom tend to change daily, weekly, or monthly, try this! Title a sheet of poster board "Free-Time Choices" and laminate it. Use a wipe-off marker to list current choices on the chart; then add and remove activities as desired. To further customize the chart, attach small Velcro strips along the left-hand margin of the chart. Laminate a supply of small cutouts, attach a Velcro strip to the back of each one, and display a cutout in front of each listing. To temporarily eliminate an activity from the chart, remove its cutout. This option is handy when noise level is a concern or when you wish to limit the activities to a specific subject area, like math-related free-time activities during math time.

LeeAnne Bohleke—Gr. 3, Charlotte Anderson Elementary, Arlington, TX

Kinsey

Bonus Pages

Monthly Booklets

Students love this free-time activity because it's fun for them to do. Teachers love it because skills are reinforced and it's easy to implement! Each month, have every child personalize a construction paper folder and title it "Bonus Pages." Each day or two place copies of a different fun-to-complete skill sheet at a free-time center. In another location, provide a completed copy of the page(s) for students to check their work by. A student with free time takes a copy of the page to his desk. When he completes the activity, he checks his work against the provided answer key, and then he stores the page in his folder. At the end of the month, help each student staple his free-time work inside his folder before he takes it home to share with his family.

Janet Finley Landry—Gr. 3
Kim Cosgrove—Gr. 3
Wren Hollow Elementary, Ballwin, MO

Quiet Transition

Stuffed animals can help make classroom transition times quiet times. Keep a collection of stuffed animals handy. When you call students together for storytime, ask your student of the week to observe his classmates and identify five or more youngsters who move to the area quickly and quietly. Then have him present each of these students with a stuffed animal that he may hold while the story is being read.

Kerry Ojeda
Paul Ecke Central School
Encinitas, CA

Make Every Minute Count

Keep five-minute fillers at your fingertips with this handy storage tip! Photocopy, cut out, and mount your favorite time-filler activities onto individual index cards. Hole-punch the cards and bind them on a large metal or plastic ring. Continue adding to the collection as desired. The next time you have a few minutes between activities, reach for your ring of favorite time fillers. Your spare minutes quickly become teachable moments!

Donna Gregory
Hodge Elementary

Transition Time Tally

This transition plan promotes teamwork and provides practice counting tally marks. Have each group (or row) of students choose a team name. List the names in the corner of the chalkboard. Each time a team makes a smooth transition between activities, draw a tally mark by its name. When a team earns 15 (or more) tally marks, recognize the team's efforts with a round of applause and, if desired, give each team member a sticker or other small reward. Then erase that team's tallies and challenge the team to earn another set!

Candi Deal
Dalton, GA

Crickets	ЖІ
Ladybugs	ЖІ І
Bumblebees	ІІІІ
Grasshoppers	ЖІ
Dragonflies	ЖІ І

Happy Birthday,

Here is my birthday wish for you:

From:

©The Education Center, Inc. • *500 Classroom Tips* • TEC60848

Happy Birthday,

Here is my birthday wish for you:

From:

©The Education Center, Inc. • *500 Classroom Tips* • TEC60848

Awards

Use with "The Clean Desk Fairy" on page 14.

Name _____

Date _____

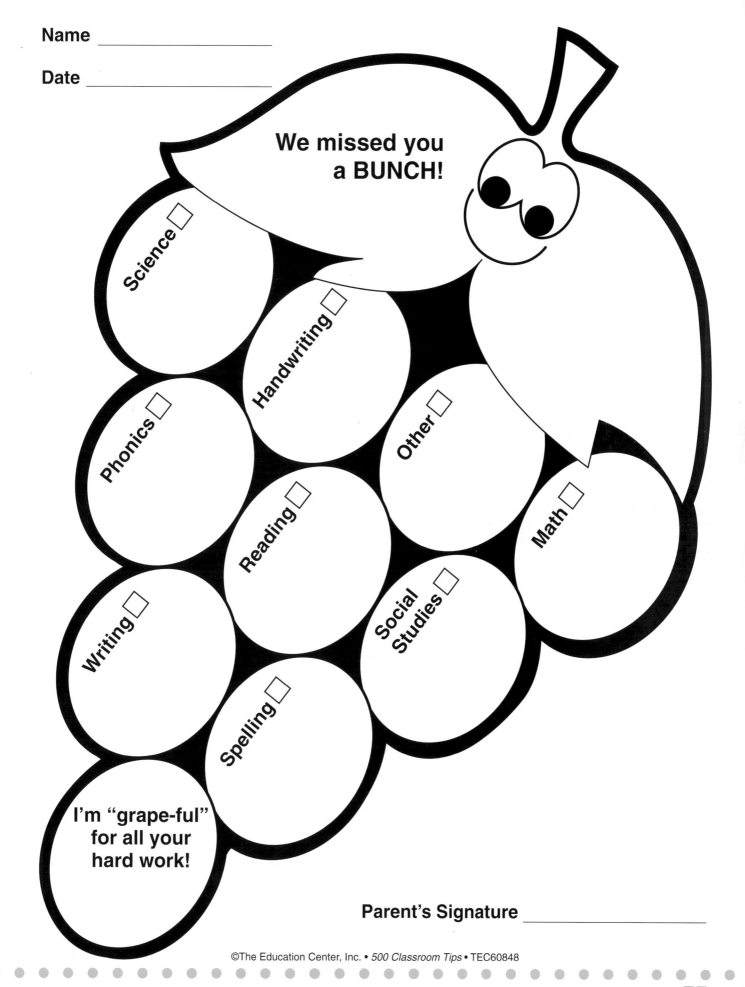

Note to the teacher: Use with "Absent Folders" on page 19.

Homework for Parents

Parent: _____ Child: _____

To help prepare for the upcoming conferences, please answer any or all of the questions below. Use the back of this sheet if more space is needed. Return this form to school no later than _____. Thanks for your comments and questions!

1. How does your child currently feel about school? _____
_____

2. How often do you and your child discuss school, and what do you discuss?
_____

3. What school subject does your child enjoy the most? _____
_____

4. What are your feelings about your child's homework assignments? _____
_____

5. Where and when does your child usually do his/her homework? And what kind of
homework assistance do you give? _____
_____
_____

6. What, if any, schoolwork has your child expressed concern about? _____
_____

7. What concerns, if any, do you have about your child's interactions with teachers
and/or other students? _____
_____

8. In what ways can I help you and your child? _____
_____
_____

9. What questions would you like to have answered at our conference? _____
_____
_____

Note to the teacher: Use with "Homework for Parents" on page 22.

My Report Card

Name: _____

Date: _____

This is how I would describe my schoolwork:

Subject	Descriptive word or phrase	This is how I plan to improve in this area
reading		
spelling		
writing		
math		
science		
social studies		

This is the subject I like the most and why: _____

_____

This is the subject I like the least and why: _____

_____

This is the special class or activity I like the most and why: _____

_____

This is how I would describe my behavior: _____

_____

I am having a problem with _____

_____

What I like best about myself is _____

_____

©The Education Center, Inc. • *500 Classroom Tips* • TEC60848

Note to the teacher: Use with "Student-Graded Report Card" on page 23.

59

Field Trip Information

Place:_____

Contact person:_____ Phone: _____

Address: _____

Recommended student ages: _____

Adult/student ratio:_____

Length of tour: _____

Admission fee: _____

Information packet available? _____

_____ bathrooms   _____ telephone   _____ tour guide
_____ first aid   _____ picnic area   _____ access for the disabled
_____ free parking   _____ bus parking   _____ gift shop
_____ other: _____

Programs offered: _____

_____

Comments: _____

_____

©The Education Center, Inc. • *500 Classroom Tips* • TEC60848

We're Going on a Field Trip!

On _____, _____ , we are
          (day)   (date)

planning a field trip to _____.

Please sign and return this note by _____
                                         (date)

so your child may participate in this learning experience.

_____ has my permission to
       (child's name)

participate in the field trip mentioned above.

_____   _____
        (date)   (parent's signature)

☐ Yes, I would like to accompany the group as a chaperone.

Please call me at _____.
                            (phone number)

©The Education Center, Inc. • *500 Classroom Tips* • TEC60848

Dear Parent,
    Our class will be having several parties this year. If you would be willing to donate a refreshment or supply item for one of our parties, please indicate your choice below and complete the remainder of the form. Return the form to school as soon as possible. Your response will be placed on file, and I will contact you several days before your donation is needed. Thank you in advance for your generosity.

Sincerely,

I would be willing to donate the following:

☐ _____ ☐ _____

☐ _____ ☐ _____

☐ _____ ☐ _____

My child's name: _____

My name: _____

Home phone number: _____

©The Education Center, Inc. • *500 Classroom Tips* • TEC60848

Dear Parent,
    Our class will be having several parties this year. If you would be willing to donate a refreshment or supply item for one of our parties, please indicate your choice below and complete the remainder of the form. Return the form to school as soon as possible. Your response will be placed on file, and I will contact you several days before your donation is needed. Thank you in advance for your generosity.

Sincerely,

I would be willing to donate the following:

☐ _____ ☐ _____

☐ _____ ☐ _____

☐ _____ ☐ _____

My child's name: _____

My name: _____

Home phone number: _____

©The Education Center, Inc. • *500 Classroom Tips* • TEC60848

Parent Note
Use with "Oops! Notice" on page 35.

Oops! Notice

Date _____

Dear _____,

    I forgot to turn in my homework today. My assignment was _____ _____.

    Please sign and date this form. I must return it with my completed homework assignment on _____.
       day of the week   date

Love,

_____
Student Signature

_____
Parent Signature

_____
Date

Oops! Notice

Date _____

Dear _____,

    I forgot to turn in my homework today. My assignment was _____ _____.

    Please sign and date this form. I must return it with my completed homework assignment on _____.
       day of the week   date

Love,

_____
Student Signature

_____
Parent Signature

_____
Date

Name _____

Homework Assignments

Week of _____

Check off each assignment as you complete it. Return this form and your assignments on Friday.

	Monday

	Tuesday

	Wednesday

	Thursday

_____
parent signature

_____
date

Note to the teacher: Use with "Homework Help" on page 35.

Incentive Charts

Use with "A Monthly Hoedown" on page 37 and "Individual Incentives" on page 38.

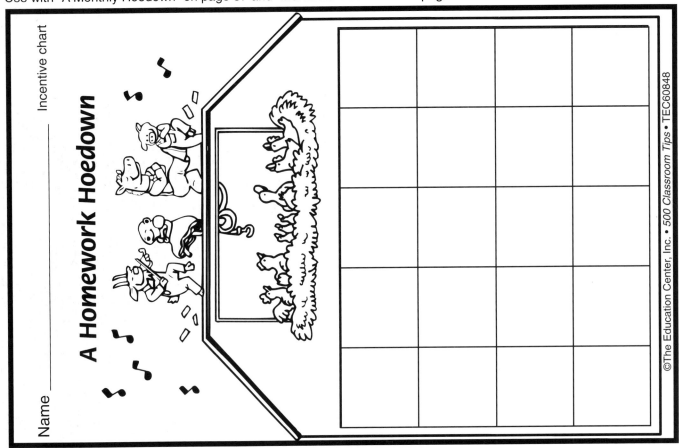

Name

Incentive chart

A Homework Hoedown

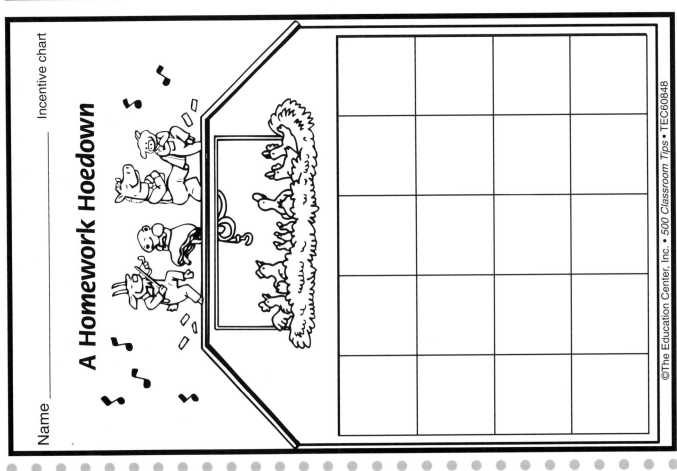

Name

Incentive chart

A Homework Hoedown

Yee-haw!

_____

has earned a
homework coupon!

(Turn in this coupon instead of
doing a homework assignment!)

Signed _____

Date _____

©The Education Center, Inc. • *500 Classroom Tips* • TEC60848

is
keeping in step
with
homework!

Signed _____

Date _____

©The Education Center, Inc. • *500 Classroom Tips* • TEC60848

Yee-haw!

_____

has earned a
homework coupon!

(Turn in this coupon instead of
doing a homework assignment!)

Signed _____

Date _____

©The Education Center, Inc. • *500 Classroom Tips* • TEC60848

is
keeping in step
with
homework!

Signed _____

Date _____

©The Education Center, Inc. • *500 Classroom Tips* • TEC60848

Conference Request

Student: _____

Concerns: _____

_____

_____

Preferred conference time: _____

Preferred day of the week: _____

_____
Parent's Signature

Conference Request

Student: _____

Concerns: _____

_____

_____

Preferred conference time: _____

Preferred day of the week: _____

_____
Parent's Signature

Conference Request

Student: _____

Concerns: _____

_____

_____

Preferred conference time: _____

Preferred day of the week: _____

_____
Parent's Signature

©The Education Center, Inc. • *500 Classroom Tips* • TEC60848

Open House Parent Questionaire

Name: ______________________________

Child's name: ______________________________

Approximate time of visit: ______________ to ______________

1. Which activity did your child seem to enjoy the most? ______________

____

____

2. Which activity did you enjoy the most? ______________

____

____

3. When did you feel most proud of your child? ______________

____

____

4. What do you think you learned from this open house experience?

____

____

Comments and/or Suggestions

____

____

____

____

____

Thank you for coming to open house! We hope you enjoyed your visit!

 Note to the teacher: Use with "Input From Parents" on page 47.

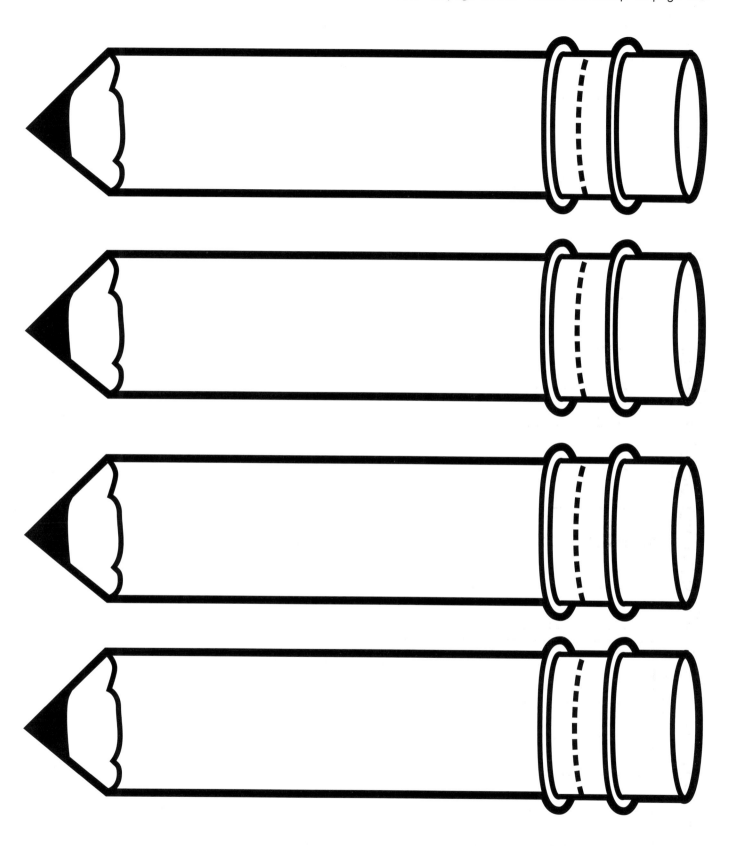

Clockface Cards

Use with "Special Classes" on page 50.

Contents

Bulletin Boards and Displays

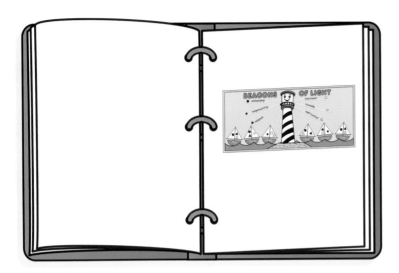

Bulletin Board Album

Keep a picture-perfect record of bulletin board ideas. Each time you decorate a bulletin board, photograph the results. Also photograph other favorite displays that you see around your school and other schools that you visit. Organize the resulting photographs in a photo album. To enhance your collection, cut out bulletin boards featured in magazines. The next time you're searching for that perfect display, you'll have an album full of good ideas to choose from!

Gayla Hammer—Grs. K–6 Life Skills
West Elementary and South Elementary
Lander, WY

Bulletin Board Snapshots

I often have difficulty recalling the layout of a bulletin board I have used in the past. To eliminate this problem. I take a photograph of each bulletin board before I disassemble the display. I store the photograph and bulletin board components together. Now I can quickly reconstruct my bulletin boards year after year.

Claudia Nisbett, Greenville, MS

Bulletin Board Binder

Find your bulletin board titles with ease! Stock a three-ring binder with top-loading plastic page protectors. Place the letters of each bulletin board title in a separate page protector and label the front of the protector with the title. Next year you'll have all your favorite bulletin board titles right at your fingertips!

Robin Wright
New Franklin Elementary School
New Franklin, MO

Border Storage

Keep a lid on additional bulletin board border purchases with this storage tip! When you remove the border from a display, roll it up and seal it inside a clean plastic container that previously contained ready-made frosting. Then label the outside of the container with a permanent marker. Your border will be ready to use and easy to find every time!

Linda L. Arnett
Peabody Elementary
Peabody, KS

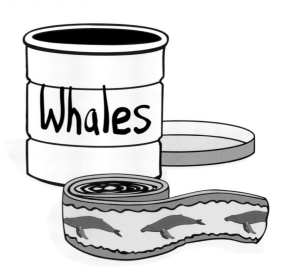

Manipulatives Coordinator

Save time by enlisting your students' help in organizing classroom manipulatives for quick and easy distribution. Every Monday assign a student to be the Manipulative Coordinator, or M.C., for the week. Each morning have the M.C. count and sort the manipulatives needed for that day. You can count on plenty of student interest in this official-sounding job.

Kim Lehmker
Our Shepherd Lutheran School
Birmingham, MI

Bag of Borders

Organizing bulletin board borders in a shoe storage bag with clear pockets is a smart idea! Suspend the bag inside a closet door. Roll up your borders and store them in the clear pockets. Now you can find the border you need at a glance!

Debra Culpepper—Gr. 3
Cedar Road Elementary
Chesapeake, VA

Bulletin Boards and Displays

Showcasing Student Work

Finding extra classroom space to display student work just got easier! Hot-glue individual clothespins to poster board stars. Use Velcro fastener, Sticky-Tac, magnetic tape, or masking tape to mount the stars on closet doors, file cabinets, windows, walls—any location that's within a youngster's reach and is suitable for displaying papers and projects. Have each child clip a sample of his finest work to a different star. Invite students to update their all-star displays as often as they wish. Everyone's a star!

Cindy Fingerlin—Gr. 3
Eisenhower School
Parlin, NJ

	Justin
1. sheep	1
2. apple	2
3. shoe	1
4. basketball	3

Eye-Catching Agenda Board

Here's a colorful way to let students know the daily schedule as they enter the classroom. Use colored chalks to draw a picture on the chalkboard that correlates with the current month or unit of study. Near the drawing, write the day's schedule along with any other important information, such as student birthdays or assignment due dates. Your students will no longer need to ask, "What are we going to do today?"

Rita Mohr—Gr. 3
South Whitley Elementary
South Whitley, IN

Book Order Box

This idea helps keep book orders from being misplaced. Set a plastic school box labeled "Book Orders" on your desk. When students return their orders to school, have them place their orders and money in the box. After mailing your class order, return the order forms to the box until the books arrive.

Jan Tschritter—Gr. 2
Linton Elementary
Linton, ND

Assignments at a Glance

Keep students aware of upcoming assignments and test dates with this visual reminder. Laminate a large calendar grid and post it on a bulletin board or wall. Each month, use a wipe-off marker to program the calendar with the month, dates, and other desired information. At a glance, students can see when assignments are due and tests will be given. At the end of the month, wipe away the programming and repeat the procedure for the succeeding month.

Ana L. Wilson
Berwyn, IL

MARCH

Mon.	Tues.	Wed.	Thurs.	Fri.	Sat.	Sun.
1	2	3 Map Due!	4	5	6 Spelling Test	7
8	9	10	11	12	13 Spelling Test	14
15	16	17	18	19	20 Spelling Test	21
22	23	24 Science Project Due!	25	26	27 Spelling Test	28
29	30 Share Projects	31 Book				

Calendar Timesaver

Tired of removing staples or masking tape each time you reposition the dates on your monthly calendar? Check your local office supply store for a "restickable" adhesive glue stick. Apply a generous coating of the adhesive to the back of calendar date cards; then press the dates on the calendar. Since the adhesive is "restickable," the dates are easy to reposition. Use the same technique to attach special messages and notes. This is a time-saver you're sure to stick with!

Barbara Turner—Gr. 3, Pelham Road Elementary, Greenville, SC

JANUARY

Mon.	Tues.	Wed.	Thurs.	Fri.	Sat.	Sun.
			1	2	3	4
5	6	7	8	9	10	11
12	13	14	15	16	17	18
19	20	21	22	23	24	25
26	27	28	29	30	31	

Remember Your Book Orders!

Here's an effective way to remind students when book orders are due. On your class calendar, attach a book-shaped cutout on the due date. At a glance, students can see the deadline for book orders.

Stephanie Speicher—Gr. 3
Elm Road Elementary School
Mishawaka, IN

Files

My File for *The Mailbox*®

As soon as you get a new issue of *The Mailbox* magazine, pull out your index cards. List each unit in the issue on a separate index card with the month and year. Then when you decide to do a unit, just glance through your alphabetical index file to find which issue to grab.

Pamela Myhowich
Auburn, WA

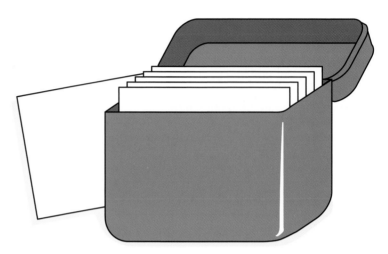

Magazine Binders

If your summer to-do list includes organizing your back issues of *The Mailbox* magazine, try this great tip. Label each of six three-ring binders for a different magazine edition. Three-hole-punch each magazine and place it in the appropriate binder in sequential order. Continue this practice each time you receive a new magazine issue. To make your binders even more usable, keep a photocopy of each end-of-the-year index at the front of your August/September binder.

Joan Hodges—Gr. 2
Lantern Lane Elementary
Missouri City, TX

Smart Stickers

As you read through each issue of *The Mailbox* magazine, label the ideas that you feel are most appropriate for your teaching situation. This can be done by attaching small stickers alongside the titles of the ideas. When you pick up the issue a few days later in search of a specific idea, turn to the desired feature or department, and you can quickly locate what you've deemed to be the best of the bunch!

Paige Murray
Academy of the Sacred Heart
St. Charles, MO

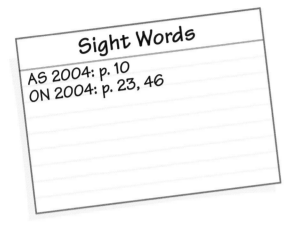

Sight Words

AS 2004: p. 10
ON 2004: p. 23, 46

The Mailbox® Magazine

If you have difficulty recalling where you saw a specific idea in *The Mailbox* magazine, try this! Label individual cards with the topics, skills, and themes that you teach. Alphabetize the cards and store them in a file box. As you read through each issue of *The Mailbox,* note each idea you're eager to use on the corresponding card in your deck. The result is a customized card catalog of ideas from *The Mailbox*!

Abbie Andrews
Wilkinson Elementary
Middleburg, FL

A Perfect Companion!

A user-friendly folder makes a perfect companion to The Mailbox Companion®, the free online service for magazine subscribers. Label the front cover of a two-pocket file folder for each magazine issue. Organize all materials printed from The Mailbox Companion inside the folder. Presto! You have more of *The Mailbox* at your fingertips!

Kelly Mitchell—Gr. 2, Van Rensselaer Elementary School, Rensselaer, IN

Organizing Back Issues

If you have difficulty remembering which topics are covered in your back issues of *The Mailbox* magazine, try this! Photocopy the table of contents from each back issue and hole-punch the copies for a three-ring binder. Label one divider page for each of the six bimonthly editions. Place the divider pages in the binder and arrange the copies of the table of contents in sequential order behind the dividers. When it's time to plan for the next school year, you'll have an invaluable resource!

Julie B. Pezzullo
Warwick School Department
Warwick, RI

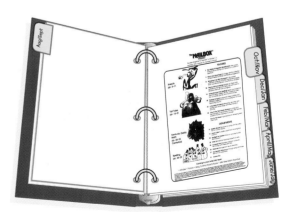

Handy Record Keeping

Gathering details about individual student performance becomes easier when you use these nifty record-keeping folders. To make a folder, label a closed file folder with the skill or behavior you wish to monitor. Inside the folder tape a class set of 3" x 5" lined index cards as shown. Label one index card per student. When you wish to record an observation, open the folder and flip to the appropriate child's card. In no time at all you'll have a wealth of information for parent conferences and report cards.

Pat Hart—Gr. 2
C. A. Henning School
Troy, IL

Follow-Up Folder

Providing individualized instruction just got easier! Keep a file folder labeled "Follow-Up Needed" on your desk. When a child's completed work indicates that he needs additional help with a skill, file his paper in the folder. Each time you have a few free minutes, select a paper from the folder and meet with the corresponding youngster. Spare minutes quickly become teachable moments!

Gina Marinelli—Gr. 2, Bernice Young Elementary, Burlington, NJ

Filing Correspondence

Minimize the risk of misplaced parent correspondence with this easy filing system. Label a file folder for each student; then alphabetically file the folders in a handy location. Whenever you receive parent correspondence (whether it be a note explaining an absence or a note of praise or concern), file the correspondence in the appropriate child's folder. If any questions arise about past parent communications, you'll have everything you need at your fingertips. The folders are also the perfect place to record your contacts with parents. To do this, attach to the inside of each folder a form that provides space for recording the date, the time, and the reason for each contact, as well as a place for jotting down the outcome of the conversation.

Alicia Stenard
Nebo Elementary
Nebo, NC

File Helpers

To help organize my files, I place a piece of colored construction paper in the front of my file folders. As I use the worksheets, I place the leftover ones in front of the construction paper. I never have to guess which papers have already been used.

Kathy Graham—Gr. 2
Filer Elementary School, Filer, ID

Identification of Copy Masters

In order to keep track of your original worksheets, punch a hole in a top corner of each page. Explain to your children that if they receive a worksheet with a hole, they should return the page to you. This simple system doesn't interfere with the quality of your copies and helps prevent the loss of your valuable copy masters.

Rosemarie Schwarz—Gr. 2, Morgan Elementary, Yardley, PA

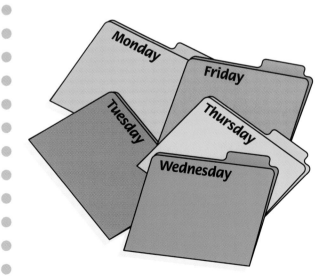

Everything for the Week

This simple idea takes only minutes on Friday afternoon, but will save you time and help you avoid last-minute confusion the following week. Label one manila folder for each day of the week. On Friday afternoon, consult your lesson plans for the coming week. Take a few minutes to gather all of the materials needed for each day. Place flash cards, charts, seatwork, etc., in the appropriate folder for the day. Your materials folder will also be a tremendous help to a substitute teacher.

Sarah Horton
Fort Payne, AL

Design a Seating Chart

Use small, self-sticking notes to make your seating chart. Laminate a 9" x 12" piece of oaktag. Label one note for each child in your class. Adhere the notes on the laminated chart to show your seating arrangement. When you change students' seats, it will be quick and easy to redo your seating plan.

Mary Dinneen
Bristol, CT

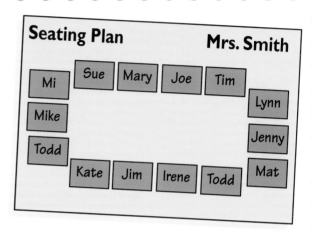

Seating Plan   **Mrs. Smith**

Mi   Sue   Mary   Joe   Tim
Mike   Lynn
Todd   Jenny
Kate   Jim   Irene   Todd   Mat

Seating Chart

Cut costs and save time with a do-it-yourself seating chart. Using a permanent marker, draw student desks on a 9" x 12" piece of oaktag; then laminate the oaktag. Write a child's name on each desk with erasable marker. To change the chart, the names wipe off and desks remain.

Mary Dinneen, Bristol, CT

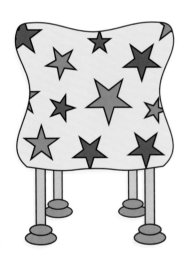

Snazzy Slipcovers

These colorful slipcovers are sure to be a hit with your next year's class. And if you purchase your fabric on sale, the cost of each slipcover is nominal. To make a slipcover that will easily fit over the back of a student's chair, cut a length of fabric that is twice the height of the chair back plus two additional inches for the hemline. The width of the fabric should equal the width of the chair back plus four additional inches. Fold the fabric in half with right sides together. Sew two half-inch side seams; then hem the bottom edge. Turn the fabric right side out and you have a ready-to-use slipcover. Sew slipcovers to recognize student birthdays, the student of the week, and your weekly table captains.

Janice Greenenwald—Gr. 2, Komarek School, North Riverside, IL

The Art of Organization

Reinforce basic art concepts while organizing your seating arrangement. Assign each of six student groups one color from the color wheel. Place a color-coded tray in the center of each group's table, and ask the groups to place their completed assignments in the trays. Name different color attributes, such as warm, cool, primary, and secondary to call on the groups for lining up, passing in papers, or gathering supplies. Or give color clues, such as "the color you get when you mix yellow and blue." Your students will listen attentively, and you'll be making the most of each teachable moment.

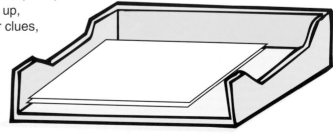

Todd Tischer—Gr. 2
Weaver Lake Elementary
Maple Grove, MN

By the Number

Score big with this classroom management tip. In the corner of each child's desktop (or table space) tape a card labeled with a numeral from 1 to 4. If student desks are arranged in groups, vary the numbers in the group. Use the numbers for a variety of tasks. For example, ask "fours" to collect math manipulatives or "threes" to line up first. Ask every "two" to pair with a "one" and so on. The possibilities are innumerable!

Lia Caprio—Gr. 3
Ingleside Elementary
Norfolk, VA

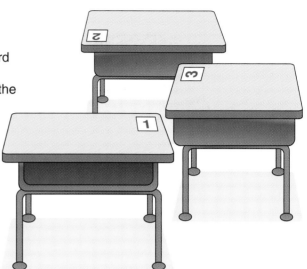

Weekday Grouping

For a practical room arrangement, organize students' desks into five groups or rows; then assign each group a different weekday name. This simple grouping lends itself to many practical uses. Refer to the group names as you call students to line up, hand in papers, or use learning centers. Each day enlist the students in that day's group to help with daily calendar activities and other classroom chores. To limit time spent on show-and-tell, have just the students in the day's group share their treasures. Students will quickly identify with their group names, making it easy for you to implement these routines and many others.

Benita Kuhlman, Avon Public School 4–1, Avon, SD

Group Captains

If your students are seated in a small-group desk arrangement, use this tip to save time *and* promote smooth transitions! In each group designate one child as the captain for the week. When it's time to collect papers or manipulatives, group members pass their materials to the captain, who then takes responsibility for the items. The group captain also distributes papers and manipulatives to the group. Establish a rotation system that allows each child a turn as captain. Along with having a more efficient classroom, you'll be nurturing responsibility!

Jeannie Hinyard—Gr. 2
Welder Elementary
Sinton, TX

Weekly Storage Box

A five-slot storage box makes weekly organization a cinch. Label each slot for one day of the school week. Store the materials needed for each day in the appropriate slot. At the end of each day, remove or refile any remaining materials.

Kathleen Hunter—Gr. 2
Tara Elementary
Forest Park, GA

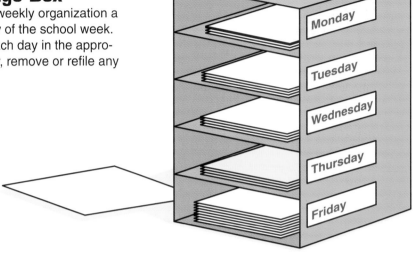

Monthly Storage

Organize your seasonal books, art ideas, and worksheets in monthly storage boxes. Label a transparent, plastic sweater container for each month of the school year; then sort your teaching materials into the boxes. Store the stackable containers in a cabinet. This system makes all of your seasonal materials easy to retrieve.

Teresa Peck, Spout Springs Elementary, Flowery Branch, GA

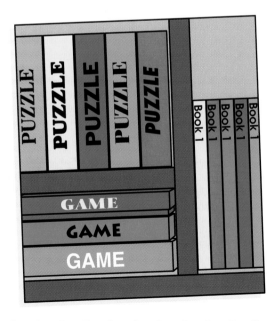

Keep It Neat

Try this tip for keeping cabinets, shelves, and learning center areas tidy. Organize and then photograph the areas of your classroom that often become cluttered. Mount the snapshots in the corresponding areas. When children return games, puzzles, books, and other supplies to these areas, they can refer to the snapshots for proper placement of the returned items. It works like a charm! The photographs will also come in handy when you are setting up your classroom next fall.

Alyce Pearl Smith
Butzbach Elementary
Germany

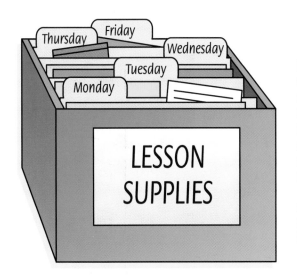

Handy Supplies

Valuable time is often spent looking for misplaced supplies. Here's a way to keep a week's worth of reproducibles, books, activities, and other fileable materials at your fingertips. Keep a file-folder organizer near your desk. Label each of five file folders with a different day of the workweek and place each folder in a separate compartment in the organizer. After you complete your lesson plans each week, stock the organizer with the needed supplies. Now when it's time to begin a lesson, your materials will be easily located.

Heidi L. Hoffman
Pershing Elementary
Lincoln, NE

Pocket Paper Organizer

There never seems to be enough time to get papers graded at school. Here's a convenient way to organize and transport your students' papers. Provide a set of stackable trays for your class. Throughout the day have students put their completed papers in the appropriate trays. At the end of the day, put each set of papers into a pocket of a spiral portfolio. Reserve one pocket to store grading materials such as pens, stickers, and answer keys. Take your organizer to appointments and on errands, and fit in some grading while you wait.

Sue Fichter—Gr. 2, St. Mary's School, Des Plaines, IL

Student Information Spirals

As you correct papers, keep track of your students' strengths and weaknesses in a spiral notebook. Label an index tab for each child and affix it to the edge of a page. Allow two or three pages for comments about each child. When you discover that a child is excelling or having difficulty with a particular skill, make note of it in the notebook. Your notes will be a great help as you prepare for conferences and report cards.

Carol A. Loveland
Randall Consolidated School
Bassett, WI

Tackling Organization

Fishing for a way to get organized? A tackle box may be just what you need! Tackle boxes come in a variety of sizes, and some models even have adjustable compartments. Sort and store your overhead supplies inside the compartments of a small tackle box. Or stock a large tackle box with paper-grading supplies like rubber stamps and stamp pads, stickers, and colorful pens. You may also want to keep a tackle box near your desk for sorting paper clips, safety pins, and other odds and ends. If you're scrambling to get organized, this "reel-y" good idea is a great catch!

Peggy McAllister—Gr. 2
Kluckhohn Elementary
Oyens, IA

See-Through Storage

Storing math manipulatives just got easier! Invite students to bring to school clean and empty plastic peanut butter jars with lids. Store math manipulatives inside the jars. Since the manipulatives are in plain sight, no labeling is required!

Sheila Criqui-Kelley
Lebo Elementary
Lebo, KS

Organizing Rubber Stamps

Clear, plastic picture frames make perfect storage containers for those sometimes messy rubber stamps. The frames are inexpensive, stackable, and easy to clean. In addition, a quick glance reveals which stamps are stored inside each frame.

Debbie Dickinson—Multiage Grs. 2–3
Libbey Elementary School
Wheatland, WY

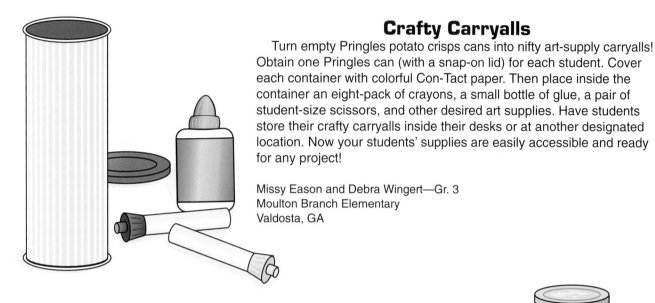

Crafty Carryalls

Turn empty Pringles potato crisps cans into nifty art-supply carryalls! Obtain one Pringles can (with a snap-on lid) for each student. Cover each container with colorful Con-Tact paper. Then place inside the container an eight-pack of crayons, a small bottle of glue, a pair of student-size scissors, and other desired art supplies. Have students store their crafty carryalls inside their desks or at another designated location. Now your students' supplies are easily accessible and ready for any project!

Missy Eason and Debra Wingert—Gr. 3
Moulton Branch Elementary
Valdosta, GA

Get on the Ball About Storage

Here's a handy classroom storage tip! Collect a large supply of clear, plastic tennis-ball canisters. (A local tennis club is a good source for rounding these up in a hurry.) For general classroom use, store chalk, pencils, art supplies, or manipulatives in the easy-view containers. Have students store their school supplies in individual tennis-ball tubes. The canisters are durable, take up less desk space than traditional pencil boxes, and are appealing to kids. So get on the ball and start gathering an assortment of tennis-ball tubes today!

Ann Marie Stephens
George C. Round Elementary, Manassas, VA

Organizing Stickers

Here's an idea that you can bank on. Keep your incentive stickers categorized with a check organizer that is divided into months. In each monthly divider, place stickers appropriate for that month. No more sorting through Christmas trees and jack-o'-lanterns to find your end-of-the-year stickers.

Ann Senn
Welch Elementary
West Monroe, LA

Storage

Textbook Storage

Do your youngsters' desks provide adequate storage space for their textbooks and other needed supplies? If not, then this tip is for you. To create extra storage space, ask each student to bring to school an empty laundry detergent box with handles. Remove the lids and cover the boxes with colorful Con-Tact paper. (This step could also be completed by your students' parents.) Have students set the boxes on the floor near their desks and use them for textbook storage. Students can use the additional space inside their desks to store other school supplies.

Sussie Brock—Gr. 3
Sugar Creek Elementary
Bentonville, AR

Classroom Library

Stick with this system and maintaining an orderly library will be as easy as A, B, C! Gather a supply of paint sticks (often free where paint is sold) and personalize one stick per student. Each time a student removes a book from the classroom library, she leaves her personalized paint stick in its place. She then removes the stick when she returns the book to its original location.

Linda Macke—Gr. 2, John F. Kennedy School, Kettering, OH

Sticker Solution

A 12-pocket expanding file with an elastic cord closure makes sticker organization a breeze! Label one pocket for each month of the school year. Label each leftover pocket with a desired theme or category. Then file your stickers accordingly. Stick with this idea and time-consuming sticker searches are over!

Cindy Schumacher
Prairie Elementary School
Cottonwood, ID

Award Binder

Organize your supply of student awards and certificates in a three-ring binder. Place copies of like awards into 9" x 12" plastic protectors. Tape the lower edge of each protector closed; then sort the awards into categories such as good behavior, neatness, and academic achievement. Label a tabbed divider page for each category. Organize the divider pages and protected awards in a binder. When you need an award, open the binder to the appropriate category and make your selection.

Laura Mihalenko—Gr. 2
Truman Elementary School
Parlin, NJ

Clutter-Busting Binder

Does it seem as though endless piles of memos and notices end up on your desk? You need a clutter-busting binder! In a three-ring binder place dividers that you have labeled with appropriate topics like "class rosters," "custodial forms," "parent correspondence," and "office memos." Alphabetize the topics for easy reference. When you receive a notice or memo, immediately file it in your binder. Not only will you be more organized, but you'll also be able to see the top of your desk again!

Nancy Lyde, Kiker Elementary School, Austin, TX

Bag It!

This timesaving idea will suit any busy teacher. You need a clear, plastic suit bag labeled for each month (or season) of the school year. When you take down your end-of-the-year classroom decorations, store them in the appropriate suit bag along with any other oversized (or hard-to-store) teaching materials for that time of year. Then sort the classroom decorations and over-sized teaching materials that are stored elsewhere in the classroom into the labeled bags. Suspend the bags in a classroom closet. Just think of the time you'll save next year when you have a clear view of each bag's contents!

Denise Baumann—Gr. 2
Rustic Oak Elementary
Pearland, TX

Color-Coded Letter Storage

Keeping letter cutouts organized is as easy as A, B, C! Sort letters by color and place each set in an expandable hanging file folder. Color each folder tab to match the letters inside; then file the folders in a plastic crate. Presto! Colorful letter cutouts at your fingertips!

Julie Decker—Gifted Grs. 1–5
Abbotsford Elementary
Abbotsford, WI

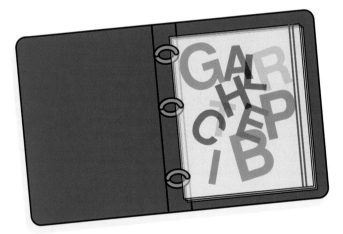

Letter Cache

Organizing letter cutouts is a snap with a letter cache. Sort your precut letters by patterns and/or sizes. Using a three-hole punch, punch holes in a supply of large Ziploc bags. Place each set of cutouts in a bag; then snap the bags into a binder. When you need letters for a bulletin board, flip through the bags until you find the set you need. This handy system also works well for organizing stickers or other small, flat items.

Ann H. Balderson—Gr. 2
Andrew Cushman School
Dartmouth, MA

Earth-Friendly Storage

Follow these easy steps to create a collection of earth-friendly storage tubs. To make a tub like the one shown, cut away the top portion of a clean one-gallon plastic milk jug—leaving the handle attached. Give each table of youngsters a storage tub to decorate. These handy tubs can be used to store math manipulatives, crayons, or supplies for a special project. Or have each table use its tub as a receptacle for small pieces of trash that would otherwise clutter the floor. The possibilities are endless!

Kathie Lloyd
Heritage Elementary
Pueblo West, CO

Organization Is a "Shoe-In"

It can be difficult to keep track of the items your students bring to you each morning. With this idea, the solution to this problem is in the bag! Hang a plastic shoe organizer with see-through pockets within reach of your youngsters. Write each student's name on a different pocket. When a student has something that needs to be given to you, he can simply place it in his plastic pocket. The item will be there until you find time to retrieve it.

Cindy Wood
Cedar Lake Christian Academy
Biloxi, MS

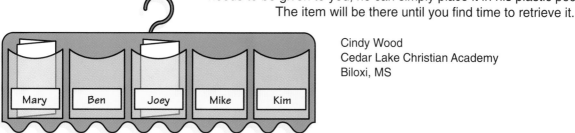

Shoe Organizer Storage

Shoe organizers with see-through pockets provide excellent classroom storage. Hang an organizer inside a closet door and store pipe cleaners, pom-poms, cotton balls, and other art supplies in the pockets. An organizer attached to a magnetic bulletin board is also perfect for holding chalk, manipulatives, hall passes, and other miscellaneous items. Materials are always in view and right at your fingertips!

Geniene Moore—Gr. 3
North Columbia Elementary
Appling, GA

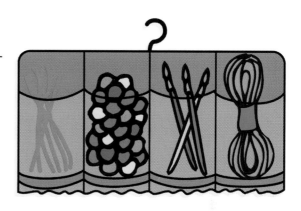

Storing Supplies

Put an end to students fishing through their desks looking for hidden supplies. Personalize a resealable plastic bag for each student; then punch a hole in each bag directly below its seal. Have each youngster seal the supplies he does not use on a daily basis inside his bag. Use metal rings to suspend the bags from plastic clothes hangers—one hanger per row or group of student desks. Store the hangers in an easily accessible location. When the supplies are needed, select students to retrieve and distribute the supply bags for their groups.

Margaret Ann Rhem—Gr. 3
Western Branch Intermediate
Chesapeake, VA

Organizing Your Classroom Library

Put your classroom books in order with this organizational tip. Group books by subjects such as fiction, nonfiction, and holidays. For each group of books, attach adhesive dots of the same color to the book spines. This system not only keeps your bookshelves organized, but also helps students identify different types of literature.

Mary Jo Kampschnieder—Gr. 2
Howells Community Catholic School
Howells, NE

Classroom Book Display

You'll be hooked on this terrific way to display paperback books in your classroom. Numerically program a set of self-adhesive hooks; then program a Ziploc bag and a paperback book to correspond with each hook. Attach the hooks to the wall. Slip each paperback into its corresponding bag; then punch a hole near the top of the bag and hang it on the corresponding hook. This display keeps books in clear view and helps you and your students see at a glance which books are missing.

Janet Zeek, South Elementary, Eldon, MO

No More Clutter

To help keep the clutter out of my classroom, I ask each student to bring in a large detergent box in which to store her school supplies. I cut a diagonal opening and cover the box with Con-Tact paper. The boxes can be stored upright with students' names prominently written on the sides.

Tami Smith—Spec. Ed. Resource Teacher
Canton, GA

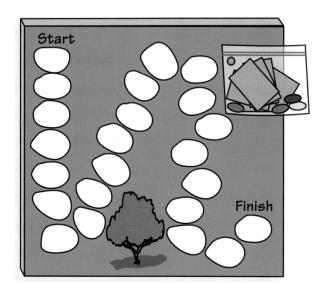

Start

Finish

Game Organization

Do you have difficulty keeping game components with their corresponding gameboards? Then this idea is for you! Using a hole punch, punch a hole in the corner of a Ziploc bag (beneath the seal) and in the corresponding gameboard. Attach the bag to the gameboard with a brad. Store game components in the bag and you'll have everything you need at your fingertips!

Terriann P. Bonfini
Bellaire, OH

Rx for Beloved Games

Game boxes can quickly become worn and torn—long before the games themselves. When this occurs, cut the directions from a game box and store the directions and the game pieces in a heavy-duty Ziploc bag. If necessary, reduce the game directions on a photocopier before placing them in the bag. Store the repackaged games in a large box. The games will have new appeal and take up less space on your game shelf!

Mary Dinneen—Gr. 2, Mountain View School, Bristol, CT

Organizing Game Pieces

Keep game pieces organized with this storage tip. Attach two matching sticky dots: one to a gameboard and the other to one drawer of a small, plastic storage chest. Label each pair of dots with the same number. Store all of the game's pieces in the labeled drawer. Organizing all of your gameboards and game pieces in this manner makes it easy for students to find the pieces they need to play each game.

Robin Woodson—Gr. 3
James Poole Elementary
Gilmer, TX

Bingo Bags

Passing out bingo markers is in the bag! For each student, place a supply of bingo markers in a Ziploc bag. When it's time to play bingo, give each student a bag of markers along with a card. When bingo time is over, have each student return his markers to the bag. Collect and store the cards and markers for later use. Now bingo materials can be passed out at a moment's notice.

Drusilla F. Warf—Gr. 2
Bluewell Elementary
Bluefield, WV

Math-O!

6	10	22	31	42
5	15	26	33	44
8	16	☺	35	46
2	19	28	36	48
1	20	30	38	50

Bingo!

Cut down on the time it takes to set up a game of bingo. Collect a class supply of empty 35mm film canisters. Fill each canister with 25–30 plastic bingo chips; then distribute a canister to each student. When it's time to play bingo, each child retrieves the canister from his desk while you distribute the cards. "Bingo!" You're ready to play!

Glenn Coolong—Gr. 2, Quarry Hill Community School, Monson, MA

Multipurpose Marker Tops

Before you toss a dried-up marker or an empty bottle of food coloring in the wastebasket, remove the colorful plastic top. Recycle these colorful tops to use as
- tokens for board games
- manipulatives for color sorting or counting activities
- materials for making finger puppets
- nonstandard units for measuring activities

Karen Spooner
Georgian Heights School
Columbus, OH

New Student Strategy

As you ready your classroom for the start of school, prepare for new student arrivals later in the year. Label each of several gallon-size plastic bags "New Student." Every time you label an item for individual students (such as a nametag, a lunch count stick, a cutout for the helper display, and a work folder), place an unlabeled item in each plastic bag. When a new student arrives, a smooth transition into her new classroom is in the bag!

Lu Brunnemer
Eagle Creek Elementary
Indianapolis, IN

Nifty Nametags

Stick with this idea and you'll receive rave reviews from substitute teachers, guest speakers, and field trip chaperones. Use a computer to label several class sets of adhesive nametags. Keep a set or two in your substitute folder and then store the rest in a handy location for easy distribution. You'll save time and minimize confusion for everyone who is involved!

Sandy Preston—Gr. 2, North Street Elementary, Brockway, PA

New-Student Checklist

When a new student arrives, you want to make him feel welcome, but it's easy to be overwhelmed by all the tasks at hand. A new-enrollee checklist may be just what you need! Design a checklist that includes a list of places where the student's name must be written, the textbooks he needs, parent information to be sent home, etc. Keep several copies of the checklist on a clipboard. When a new student arrives, refer to the checklist to help you take care of all the necessary details as quickly as possible. You'll have the new student settled into your class in no time!

Kristin Moyer—Gr. 2
Weigelstown Elementary
Dover, PA

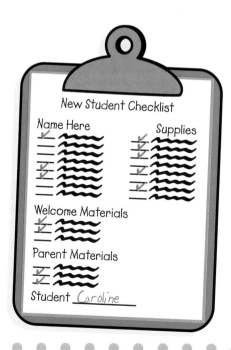

Instant Anecdotes

Write anecdotal records quickly and efficiently with this instant system. Keep a supply of computer disk labels handy. Whenever you wish to record a child's involvement in a classroom occurrence, simply jot it down on a label along with the child's name and date. Later each label can be transferred easily to a notebook, card file, or permanent record.

Patricia J. Hamilton
Kempsville Elementary
Virginia Beach, VA

The Borrow Box

Here's an easy way to keep track of classroom materials that you've lent to other teachers. Each time an item is borrowed, write its name and the borrower's name on a small index card. Store the card in a file box. When an item is returned, cross the borrower's name off the card.

Gayla Hammer—Grs. K–6 Life Skills: Special Education
West Elementary & South Elementary
Lander, WY

Whose Project Is Whose?

When making art or food projects which involve baking, it's often difficult to remember which child made each project. To avoid mix-ups, lay waxed paper on your baking sheet. Then as students place their projects on the sheet, write their initials on the waxed paper next to their projects.

Debbie Schneck
Schnecksville, PA

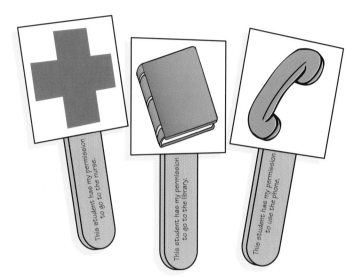

Hall Passes

Use tongue depressors for handy hall passes. Tape a picture of a nurse, telephone, or library book to the sticks. Write a message on each stick, such as "This student has my permission to use the phone." Put magnetic tape on the backs of the passes, and store them on your filing cabinet.

Connie Connely
Catoosa Elementary
Catoosa, OK

Favorite Reproducibles

If you're always scrambling to locate your tried-and-true reproducibles, try organizing them with this great tip. You will need a three-ring binder with dividers. Label one divider for each month of the school year. Three-hole-punch your favorite reproducibles (student activities, parent letters, party notices) and place them in the binder according to the month in which they will be used. Your reproducibles will be right at your fingertips when you need them.

Cheryl Sneed, Winters Elementary, Winters, TX

A Timesaving Investment

Do you spend too much of your valuable time writing your name on school correspondence? Here's a quick-and-easy way to label book orders, newsletters, parent information sheets, attendance forms, etc. All you need is an inexpensive rubber stamp imprinted with your name and the name and address of your school. One quick application and your name is clearly printed on your correspondence. Parents find this beneficial as well. If they have more than one student in school, it's easy to see to which child a note from school belongs.

Pam Gunter—Gr. 2
Jupiter Elementary
Palm Bay, FL

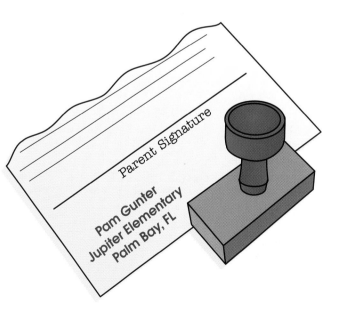

Supplies

No More Glitter Litter!
Glitter—your students love it, but you don't like the mess. Here's the solution! Before sprinkling glitter onto artwork, place a box lid underneath the art. The lid catches the loose glitter. When finished, simply pick up the lid,, tap the glitter into a corner, and pour it back into the original container.

Kathy Mobbs
Farmington, MI

Scrap Art
Construction paper scraps—they're as valuable as gold to a classroom of young artists! Introduce your students to the works of a famous artist or designer such as Pablo Picasso or Frank Lloyd Wright. After sharing pictures of the artist's work, give each student a supply of paper scraps, a pair of scissors, a piece of art paper, and glue. Have the child cut out and glue the scraps to the paper to create a work of art in the style of the featured artist. Mount the finished projects on poster board or—better yet—old manila file folders. Move over, Monet!

Linda Maxwell, Edgewood Elementary, Birmingham, AL

Art Supply Center
A little advance preparation can really pay off during arts-and-crafts lessons. In each of several labeled containers, place a desired quantity of craft supplies; then place the containers on a designated shelf. When supplies are needed, they will be readily available for distribution. At the end of each lesson, return the supplies to the appropriate containers. Have one student verify the contents of each before returning them to the shelf. If desired, replenish consumable items at this time.

Tina Merdinyan
Seattle, WA

30 Paintbrushes

Apron Art Assistant

This multi-pocket apron stores supplies for independent or small group use. Hang the apron in an art center. Fill the apron pockets with pens, pencils, crayons, paper clips, scissors and tape.

Sr. Ann Claire Rhoads
Mother Seton School
Emmitsburg, MD

Glue Refills

Take this approach, and students always have glue when they need it! Near your sink or supply area, post a sign like the one shown and then confirm that each child's glue bottle is personalized. When a student is almost out of glue, she drops off her glue bottle at the filling station before she leaves for the day. Each afternoon, refill (and return) glue bottles as needed.

Sandy Preston—Gr. 2
North Street Elementary School
Brockway, PA

Large Lids

Tired of scrubbing dried glue from desktops? Here's an idea for you! Enlist your students' help in collecting large circular plastic lids. Store the lids in an easily accessible classroom location. When a student is using glue, he retrieves a large plastic lid and places it under his project to catch excess glue. If his project requires additional drying time, he uses the lid to transport the project to a convenient classroom location. Glue that dries on the plastic lids is easy to peel off. Now instead of flipping your lid over dried glue—grab one!

Linda Brandt—Gr. 2
Roundtown Elementary School
York, PA

Paint Containers

Margarine and cream cheese containers can help you avoid the spills and splatters of paint day. Put one inch of paint in each container. Cut a hole in the lid appropriate to the brush size. Replace the lid, slipping in the brush. Extra paint is wiped away when the brush is raised.

Pamela Huntington
Redington Shores, FL

Individual Paint Palettes

Take the pain out of class painting projects with individual paint palettes! Give each child a five-inch square of leftover laminating film. To disperse paint, squeeze dollops of desired tempera paints directly on the palettes. When it's time for cleanup, allow the paint on the palettes to dry before removing it (it crumbles easily). Presto! The palettes are ready to be reused!

Charlotte Cross—A.R.T.S.
Fletcher Elementary
Fletcher, OK

Stamp Pad Solution

Does your stamp pad seem to dry out too quickly? It may be that the ink has sunk to the bottom of the pad. To alleviate this problem, store your stamp pad upside down. When you're ready to use it, the ink will be near the top of the pad, and you'll get the picture-perfect stamps you're hoping for!

Christen M. Reiner
Lavaland Elementary School
Albuquerque, NM

Curriculum Ties and Lesson Helps

Contents

Centers

Parent Tutors and Learning Centers

Finding time to work with children who need individual help is a real challenge to most classroom teachers. Solve the problem by enlisting the help of parent volunteers and your collection of learning centers. Have interested parents sign up for tutoring time slots. When a parent arrives to tutor a specific student or small group, give her an appropriate learning center or game that focuses on the necessary skill. The tutor and student(s) can work quietly together while you focus on the rest of the class.

Debra Gustavson
Danbury, WI

Center Choice Board

Operate your classroom centers efficiently and effectively with a center choice board. Cut out, label, and laminate a construction paper circle for each center. Attach small Velcro squares to each center circle to indicate how many students may attend that center at one time. Display the circles.

Each student needs a marker backed with an adhesive Velcro square. When a student visits a center, he places his marker on the appropriate circle at the center choice board. If all the Velcro squares are full, he chooses a different center.

Mary A. Carl, Cary Woods School, Auburn, AL

Centers in the Round

Organize your classroom centers with this color-coded system. Tape a different-colored, laminated, construction paper apple cutout to each of your classroom centers. Then use a permanent felt-tip marker to draw lines on a pizza pan, dividing it into the number of sections that equals the number of classroom centers. Attach a colored apple cutout that corresponds with the apple on each center to each section of the pizza pan. Next, use a felt-tip marker to program a spring-type clothespin for each classroom student. Clip a desired number of the clothespins to each pizza pan section, indicating the center that each student should visit first. At the end of the day, move each child's clothespin clockwise to the next pizza pan space. When each child has had a chance to visit all the centers, change the center activities and begin again!

Carol Sokol, St. Mary's School, Avon, OH

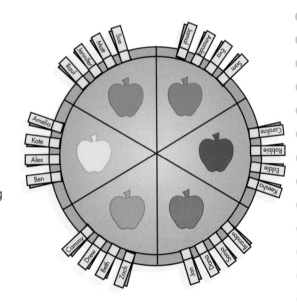

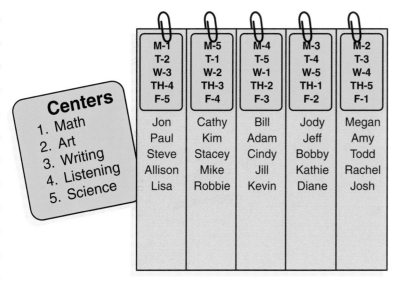

Centers
1. Math
2. Art
3. Writing
4. Listening
5. Science

M-1	M-5	M-4	M-3	M-2
T-2	T-1	T-5	T-4	T-3
W-3	W-2	W-1	W-5	W-4
TH-4	TH-3	TH-2	TH-1	TH-5
F-5	F-4	F-3	F-2	F-1
Jon	Cathy	Bill	Jody	Megan
Paul	Kim	Adam	Jeff	Amy
Steve	Stacey	Cindy	Bobby	Todd
Allison	Mike	Jill	Kathie	Rachel
Lisa	Robbie	Kevin	Diane	Josh

Center Rotation

This handy chart allows you to easily rotate groups of students to different learning centers. Divide your students into five groups. Visually divide a piece of poster board into five columns. In each column, list the members of one group. (See the illustration.) Next, label each center with a letter or number. Using this code, program a weekly center schedule for each of the five groups. Clip the schedules to the poster board chart. Display the chart and the center code side by side. To change center assignments, either rotate the existing cards or attach new cards to the chart.

Dianne Knight—Gr. 2
Frank C. Whiteley School
Hoffman Estates, IL

Center Management

If you have centers that are consistently overcrowded, try this center management chart. First, determine how many students can occupy each center at one time. Label one library pocket per center. Then label one paper strip per center occupant. Glue the library pockets to a sheet of poster board and slip the strips in the corresponding pockets. To visit a center, a student takes a paper strip labeled with the name of the center. If no strips are available, he makes another center choice. When the student completes the center, he returns the strip. Eliminating center pileups has never been easier!

Jennifer P. Gann—Gr. 2
Seymour Primary School
Seymour, TN

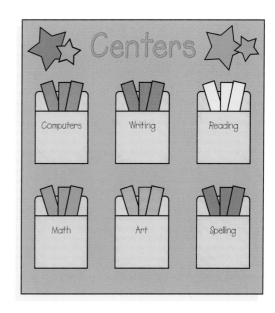

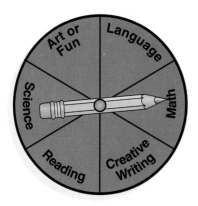

Spin-a-Center

Motivate your children to complete a variety of learning centers with a learning-center wheel. To make a wheel, divide a tagboard circle into sections. Write the name of a learning center in each section. Use a brad to attach a pencil-shaped spinner to the center of the cutout. When a child completes his assigned work, he spins the wheel to determine which center to complete.

Leigh Anne Newsom—Gr. 3, Greenbrier Intermediate, Chesapeake, VA

Choosing Centers

Prevent overcrowded learning centers with this student-managed display! Label one section of a bulletin board for each classroom center. Along the lower edge of each section, within students' reach, insert one pushpin for each child who can work at the center at one time. To visit a center, a student suspends a personalized cutout (provided for this purpose) from an unoccupied pushpin at the display. When he leaves the center, he retrieves his cutout.

Liz Robertson—Grs. K–4
Pickens Elementary
Pickens, SC

Organizing Centers

Organize materials for your daily center activities in a jiffy! Establish a color for each of your learning centers; then color-code a resealable plastic storage bag to match each center. In each center bag, place the materials that are needed to complete the center. When center time is over, ask one child at each center to seal the remaining center materials in the center bag.

Cindy Wood, Cedar Lake Christian Academy, Biloxi, MS

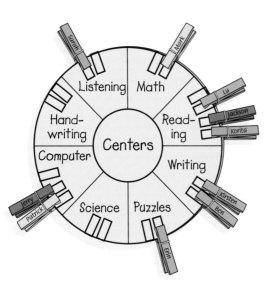

Center Selections

Here's an easy way to avoid overcrowded learning centers. Write the name of each classroom center on a poster board circle like the one shown. Along the edge of each circle section, draw one or more rectangles to show how many students can work at the center at one time. Laminate the resulting center wheel and display it within students' reach. A student clips a personalized clothespin in an empty rectangle on the center wheel and then visits the corresponding center. When she leaves the center, she removes her clothespin. It's a snap!

Mary E. Hoffmann—Gr. 2
Camp Avenue Elementary
North Merrick, NY

Picture-Perfect

Labeling classroom learning centers is easy with the help of inexpensive, clear acrylic picture frames. Write the title and directions for each learning activity on an index card; then slip each card into a different frame. Place the frames at the corresponding learning centers. When it's time to change an activity, simply slide the card out of the frame and replace it with a new set of directions. Your centers will be neat and organized, and students will easily see the directions for each activity.

Liz Kramer—Gr. 2
Boyden School
Walpole, MA

Pretty Patterns
1. Use the blocks to make a pattern.
2. Draw and color the pattern on your paper.

Center Rotation

Do your students have difficulty remembering which learning center to go to each day? Eliminate the confusion with this simple plan. Divide your students into a desired number of groups (one group per center). Assign each group a shape such as a yellow star or a blue square; then suspend each shape at a center. When a child enters the classroom, he looks for his shape and immediately knows which center to go to. Rotate the center shapes daily in a clockwise direction; then change the center activities at the end of each complete rotation. For easy management, have students keep their assigned shapes throughout the year.

Patricia J. Hamilton, Kempsville Elementary, Virginia Beach, VA

Name Jeffrey

You did a great job today! ☺

Day of the week Monday

Check Out That Center

This idea will help students remember which classroom centers they have visited. First, label each classroom center with a symbol. Next, give each student a center checklist similar to the one shown. For each center that a student visits, instruct him to put a check mark in the appropriate box. After a student has visited each classroom center, he writes his name and the day of the week on his checklist and then hands it in. You can quickly see if the student has had a chance to visit all the classroom centers; then write a note of encouragement to him.

Sandy Shaw
Jeannette McKee Elementary
Jeannette, PA

Centers

Pegboard Pleaser

Taking turns for center work is no problem using this convenient name card idea. Place an 8" x 6" pegboard into a grooved rectangular wood base. Attach two hooks to the pegboard labelled "in" and "out." Hang all student name cards on the "in" hook. When a child completes the center he moves his card to the "out" hook and taps the next person.

Lynette Stewart—Gr. 3
Woodlawn Academy
Chatham, VA

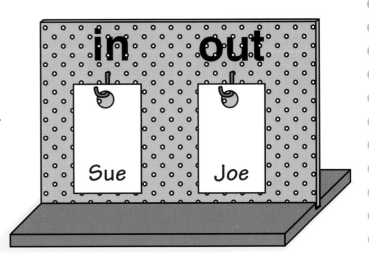

Learning Center Record Keeping

To make sure youngsters have equal opportunities to use your learning centers, try this record-keeping system. Place a class roster at each center. After completing a center, a child crosses off his name. A student may repeat a center after all of his classmates have had a chance to participate.

June Blair, Franklin Elementary School, Reisterstown, MD

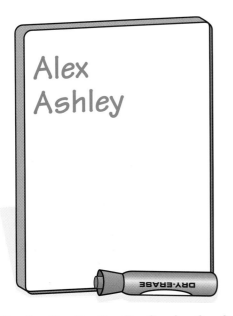

Checking Centers

Enlist the help of your students for checking learning-center work. Check the work of the first child to complete the center. If his work is correct, write the student's name on a list at the center. (If the work is not correct, continue checking student work until a correct version is identified.) When the next child completes the center, she reads the name on the list and asks that child to check her work. If her work is correct, she adds her name to the list. Each child thereafter does the same thing, having the child whose name is last on the list check her work. Children love to help their classmates and you'll love the extra time!

Linda Madron
Mary D. Lang Elementary
Kennett Square, PA

Organizing Books and Cassettes

Here's an easy way to organize books and their corresponding tapes. Sequentially number the books; then label each book's tape with a matching number. Store the books on a shelf n order. Sequentially store the cassettes nearby in a tape case. This system is so easy that children can easily locate (and return) the components of book-and-tape sets.

Jeanine Peterson—Gr. 2
Bainbridge Elementary
Bainbridge, IN

No More Tangles

This organizational tip keeps your youngsters from becoming all tangled up in your listening center. Mount a sturdy, plastic towel bar on the wall nearest your listening center. Using colored markers or adhesive dots, clearly label the headsets and the towel bar with corresponding colors. Then label the outlets at the listening center with the same color code. A student identifies the color-coded outlet that is nearest him and removes the matching headset from the bar. At the end of the activity, he returns the headset to its appropriate location.

Melana Watley
Britt David Elementary
Columbus, GA

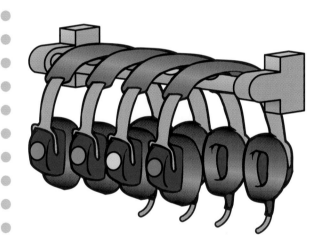

Hook a Book

Taking a few minutes now to organize your book and tape sets will prepare you for fall, plus it encourages this year's students to revisit your collection. Place each book and its corresponding tape in a resealable plastic bag and then clip a clothespin hanger to the bag. Display a sheet of pegboard near your listening center. Insert inexpensive hooks into the pegboard and suspend each bag from a hook. Your students will be all ears!

Alisa T. Daniel
Ben Hill Primary
Fitzgerald, GA

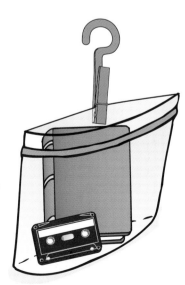

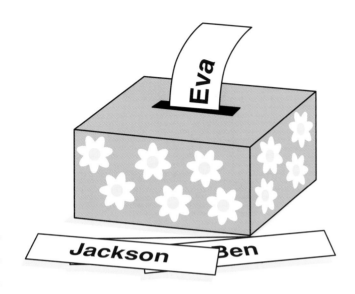

Learning Center Raffle

Your children are sure to use their free time wisely with this learning center incentive. When students complete free-time learning centers, have them write their names on slips of paper and then place the personalized slips in a class raffle box. After a designated number of weeks, draw a name from the box and present a prize to the winning child. Then empty the box and start the activity again.

Lorinda Bodiford
Souder Elementary
Everman, TX

Reproducible Gameboards

Here's a nifty way to turn a reproducible gameboard into a kid-pleasing center activity. Color the gameboard and then glue it inside a clean and empty pizza box. (For added durability, cover the gameboard with a layer of clear Con-Tact covering.) Store any required game pieces—like a spinner, dice, or game markers—inside the box. Invite a student or two to decorate the box according to the game's theme. The box increases the appeal of the game, makes the game easy to store, and provides a quiet surface for rolling dice.

Hope Harbin—Gr. 3, Hephzibah Elementary, Hephzibah, GA

Dice Mats

These easy-to-make mats muffle the sounds of rolling dice. To make the mats, cut one-foot squares from nonslip drawer lining. Store the resulting dice mats near your supply of dice. To use a mat, a student presses it flat against his playing surface. Roll 'em!

Marcia Hopkins
James Ellis Elementary
Niles, MI

The Surprise Center

Each week, place a surprise cooking, art, or hands-on activity at a large center table. Small groups of assigned students visit it daily. The children can hardly wait to find out what the surprise activity is for the week!

Sr. Mary Catherine Warehime
Holy Cross Regional School
Lynchburg, VA

Wall Organizer

To display your learning centers and file folders, attach two strips of 2½-inch wood stripping to a wall or bulletin board. Leave approximately two feet between the top and bottom strips. Place one-inch self-adhesive Velcro pieces on the stripping. Put the small Velcro pieces on the backs of your centers and attach to the stripping. Be sure to hang strips according to the height of your students.

Pizza Box Bonus

Large pizza boxes are perfect for storing center-making materials. Label the end of each box to show what it contains (patterns, wrapping paper, game pieces); then stack the boxes to save space. Pizza boxes of any size also make great center games. Unfold the boxes and program the inside areas with directions and activities. Cover the outside areas with wrapping or Con-Tact paper. (Laminate unfolded boxes if desired.) Refold the boxes and secure the sides with hot glue. Store playing pieces and cards inside. Label the box ends with center names and skills; then neatly stack. Inquire about the availability of clean boxes at your local pizza restaurant.

Shirley May
Moscow, KS

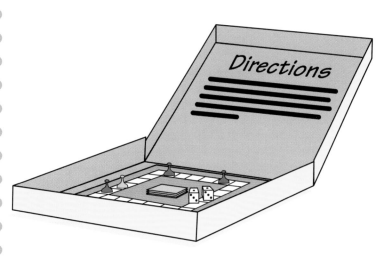

Lesson Plans

Scheduling Tip

Get a clear picture of when individual students attend special classes with this tip. Clip a sheet of clear plastic over each page of your current week's plans and then use a colorful wipe-off pen to program the plastic with desired information. (See the illustration.) Each week transfer the plastic sheet to your current plans and update as needed. A quick glance reveals who is exiting when, as well as when the entire group will be together. A substitute teacher is sure to appreciate this helpful approach.

Darcy Keough
Doolittle School
Cheshire, CT

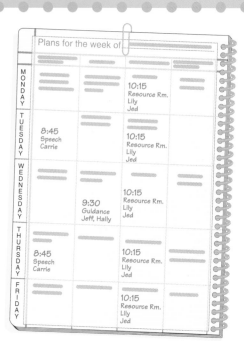

Lesson Plan Updates

Updating and reprogramming your weekly lesson plans is a snap with this slick approach! Create a weekly lesson plan format that suits your needs, and program it with times and classes that remain constant throughout the school year. Laminate the project and post it in an easily accessible location. Each week write your plans in wipe-off marker. As adjustments are needed or lessons are completed, wipe off and reprogram the weekly plan. Just think of the time you'll save this spring!

Stephanie Crawford—Gr. 2, Monticello Elementary, Tracy, CA

Lesson Plan Lists

Stick with this idea and you'll know at a glance if you have the supplies you need for each day's lessons. As you plan for the upcoming week, label one sticky note per school day. Attach the notes to the corresponding lesson plan page or to an inside cover of your planbook. On each note, list papers to duplicate, supplies to gather, and so on. Cross off the tasks as you finish them. When an entire list is completed, toss it and feel twice the satisfaction—your list is gone and your preparation is complete!

Tiffany L. Gosseen
Hopkins, MO

Creative-Writing Organizer

Keep materials for your creative-writing lessons and projects in a handy organizer. Using notebook dividers, separate a large three-ring binder into sections for the months of the school year. Slide your projects and their accompanying lesson plans and materials into clear plastic sleeves; then file the sleeves in the appropriate sections. Everything you need for successful writing instruction is at your fingertips.

Barbara Fredd—Gr. 3
Oregon City, OR

Binder Plans

Use this tip to help prepare hassle-free lesson plans. Divide a three-ring notebook into sections using subject dividers. In each section, write the lessons you plan to teach for that particular subject. After a lesson is taught, check it off. If a class period is canceled or if it is necessary to reteach a lesson, do not check off the lesson. This timesaving system eliminates the need to recopy lessons from week to week. Use this binder to assist substitutes by placing a copy of your class schedule and other important information in a front pocket.

Karyn Karr—Gr. 3, Cleveland Elementary School, Cedar Rapids, IA

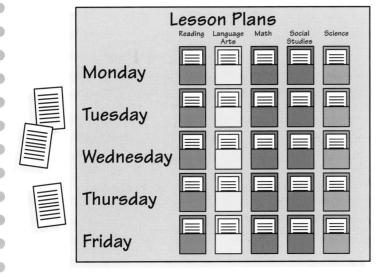

Pocket Plans

Display your weekly lesson plans with this convenient chart. On poster board, glue library card pockets in five rows as shown. Label the subjects and the days of the week. Then, on separate index cards, write your daily lesson plans for each subject. Place the cards in the appropriate pockets. To teach a lesson, remove the card from the pocket. All of the information you need is right in your hands.

Denise Johnson—Gr. 3
Lundgren School
Topeka, KS

Lesson Plans

Marked for Success

Do you find that your students have a difficult time locating pages in their textbooks? If so, this timesaving tip is for you. Make a set of personalized construction paper bookmarks for each student. Laminate the bookmarks for durability; then distribute them to students. When a lesson is over, ask students to use their bookmarks to mark the page. The next time that textbook is used, have the child open to the marked page and you're ready to begin a new lesson! For each textbook used, have students repeat this process using a different bookmark from their sets. Keep enthusiasm for this activity high by periodically rewarding students who have their bookmarks on the correct page.

Phil Forsythe—Gr. 3
Northeastern Elementary School
Bellefontaine, OH

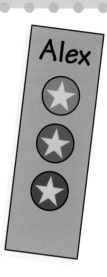

Seasonal Selections

These monthly folders take the guesswork out of knowing which seasonal activities or reproducibles you've used. Label one folder (with two inside pockets) for each month of the school year. Inside each folder, label one pocket "Ideas, Activities, and Worksheets" and one pocket "Used This Month." Slip your seasonal activities into the appropriate pockets; then store the folders in a convenient location. Each month remove the appropriate folder from storage. Throughout the month transfer the activities you use into the pocket labeled "Used This Month." At the end of the month, return the papers to their original pocket and store the folder until next year.

Diane Fortunato—Gr. 2, Carteret School, Bloomfield, NJ

Ideas, Activities, and Worksheets

Used This Month

Skill Plan

Use this handy display to keep track of which curriculum skills are being introduced, reinforced, or tested. Visually divide a portion of a classroom wall into four columns. Label the columns from left to right as follows: "New Skills," "Introduced," "Reinforced," and "Tested." Label a cutout for each curriculum skill you are responsible for teaching. Use magnets, adhesive Velcro strips, or masking tape to display the labeled cutouts in the New Skills column; then move the cutouts into the appropriate columns as the skills are being taught. Throughout the year, a quick glance at the display can tell you what skills need attention.

Cindy Sweeney—Gr. 3
Homan Elementary School
Schererville, IN

main idea

subtraction facts to 18

Sample Book

To help you remember which shapes can be created on your school's die-cut machine, make a sample book. To do this, gather one sample of each shape. Categorize the shapes as desired; then glue the shapes onto the pages of a blank booklet or spiral notebook. Use divider tabs to label the different sections of the sample book. There you have it—a shipshape sample book!

Karen Bryant—Gr. 3
Rosa Taylor Elementary
Macon, GA

Foldaway Flannelboard

Open your door to this space-saving flannelboard! Cut a rectangle of felt that is the width of your classroom doorway and a desired length plus two inches. Fold and stitch a one-inch casing across the top and bottom of the felt. Then slip a spring-style curtain rod into each casing. Position the flannelboard in your doorway and it's ready to use. To store, simply release the curtain rods and roll up the project. This portable flannelboard also makes a terrific puppet theater!

Karen Smith
Pine Lane Elementary Homeschool
Pace, FL

Planning for a Substitute

Making advance plans for a substitute is a snap with this reusable lesson planner. Write or type your daily schedule on a series of large index cards. Where appropriate, leave blank lines for writing specific information. (See illustration.) Laminate the cards. Using a hole puncher, punch a hole in the left-hand corner of each card; then bind the cards together on a metal ring. Using a wipe-off marker, write the lesson plans your substitute will need on the cards. When you return, wipe away the programming and store the lesson planner for future planned absences.

Chris Noel—Gr. 3
Monrovia Elementary School
Monrovia, IN

Regrouping for Math

If you frequently need to regroup students for math lessons to meet specific objectives, individual student nametags will make your job easier. Attach a self-adhesive magnetic strip to the back of each nametag; then group the tags on a magnetic board or file cabinet. A student can quickly tell which math group he should attend by glancing at the nametag display. When you need to regroup the students, just rearrange the tags.

Sandra Gray—Gr. 3
Woodfield Elementary School
Gaithersburg, MD

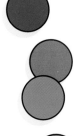

Color-Coding Tips

Color-coding the materials for each of your math and reading groups will save you time answering questions. Use these tips to get started:

- Color-code reproducibles with dots or permanent markers so students can easily find them.
- Color-code storage boxes so students can put their work in the correct place.
- Color-code flash cards by clipping them together with a big colored clip, or make the first flash card in each deck a color.
- Duplicate reproducibles on colored paper.
- If you are doing a special unit with one group, color-code all resource materials for that group.
- Color-code learning centers, games, and file folders for each group.

Sister Ann Claire Rhoads, Mother Seton School, Emmitsburg, MD

Hop to It!

Get each child leaping ahead on learning the times tables with this lily pad bulletin board. Each child has a frog with his or her name on it. As a table is mastered, the child moves his frog to that lily pad. Give special awards after each leap and an extra special award for getting across the entire pond.

Christine Davidson
Marietta, GA

Manipulative Math Bags

Do you spend precious minutes of math time distributing and collecting manipulatives? Try this! Personalize a large zippered bag for each child. Every week or so, stock the bags with the manipulatives students need for the next several math lessons. Store the bags in a designated container and distribute them as needed. Or ask each child to store her math bag inside her desk. Every minute saved is one more minute of math instruction!

Kimberly Baker
Skyview Elementary
Richardson, TX

Daily Math Warm-Up

Spotlight the current date and review math skills with this opening activity. Each morning, challenge students to create math problems that total the day's date. Write the student-generated problems on the chalkboard. Since students create the problems themselves, each child can adjust the difficulty level of her problem to match his capabilities. This results in a fun and successful math review for everyone involved!

Leta Bell—Grs. 1–3, Glenpool Elementary, Glenpool, OK

Math Challenges

This free-time math activity has three kid-pleasing options. Place three trays at a math center. Fill the first tray with blank paper, label the second tray "Problems to Solve," and label the third tray "Problems to Check." Position a fourth tray labeled "Finished Papers" near your desk. A student with free time may take a blank sheet of paper, create a page of problems for a classmate to solve, and then place the paper in the "Problems to Solve" tray. Or she may complete a paper from the "Problems to Solve" tray and place it in the "Problems to Check" tray. Another option is to correct a paper from the "Problems to Check" tray and then place the completed paper in the "Finished Papers" tray. So many options and so much math. Now that adds up to a great free-time opportunity.

Karen Lee Koroluk—Grs. 2–3, St. Dominic Savio Elementary, Regina, Saskatchewan, Canada

Monthly Workmats

Protect desktops and strengthen calendar skills with monthly workmats! Each month, have every child program a blank calendar grid for the current month and label it with family- and school-related events. Next, have him glue the calendar on a 12" x 18" sheet of construction paper, personalize the project, and add desired artwork. Laminate the completed mats. Ask students to work atop their mats when they use potentially messy supplies such as glue and paint. The end result is cleaner desktops and more calendar-related conversations!

Betty Klein, Sheridan Road School, Fort Sill, OK

Start the Day With a Graph

Make this graph activity a part of your students' daily school routine. Each morning when students arrive, have a question printed on the chalkboard. Underneath the question have a bar graph with a variety of answers from which the students can choose. Have each student use chalk or a personalized sticky note to mark her response to the question. (If you have a magnetic bulletin board, provide each student with a magnetic name card that can be placed in a bar-graph column of the student's choice.) When the graph is complete, challenge each student to write five conclusions and/or questions about the information gathered from the graph. Did you know that eight of our classroom students have five letters in their first names?

Debra Fitzgerald, Badger Road Elementary, Fairbanks, AK
Toby B. Grosswald, Olney Cluster School, Philadelphia, PA

Computer Lab Queries

Implement this three-step approach to answering computer-related questions and there's an excellent chance students will use it throughout the school day! Ask that during lab time each child try first to answer his own question. If he cannot, he asks a classmate for help. If his question is still unanswered, he displays a bright orange card (or something similar) to request help from the teacher. Along with fostering a user-friendly lab, you'll boost the self-esteem of your students!

Cori Collins—Computer Teacher K–5
St. Mary, St. Margaret Mary, and St. Gabriel Schools
Neenah-Menasha; WI

Using an Overhead

This activity will brighten a rainy day! Select reproducible pages from *The Mailbox* magazine to use for making overhead transparencies. Project a transparency on the blackboard and let students take turns working the lesson on the board. My students especially enjoy pages that must be completed with colored chalk. They can't wait until the lights are turned on to see the completed picture!

Karen Wigger—Gr. 2
Maysville, MO

Teacher's Cart Caddy

Saddle up your overhead projector cart with this convenient supply caddy! Measure the width and the length of the top shelf of your cart. Using a heavy-duty material such as denim, cut out a rectangle with the following dimensions: length = the width of the top shelf plus 28 inches, width = the length of the top shelf. Machine-hem all edges. Fold up eight inches of fabric on one end and sew the outer edges together to create a large pocket. Sew a straight seam down the center of the pocket to make two smaller pockets. On the opposite end, fold up five inches of fabric and sew the outer edges together. Create three small pockets by sewing two straight seams down the resulting pocket. Drape the completed caddy over your cart, adjusting it so that pockets hang from the sides. Then place your projector on the covered shelf. With your caddy in place, you can now have your overhead supplies at your fingertips.

Donna Bean
Arthur Elementary School
Cedar Rapids, IA

5"   8"

Pizza-Box Portfolios

Do you find that file folders won't hold everything you and your students want to include in their portfolios? Then try this quick-and-easy alternative. Ask a local pizzeria to donate a class supply of large pizza boxes; then personalize a box for each student. Throughout the year, fill each student's pizza-box portfolio with samples of student work, an audiotape featuring the student's oral reading, and art projects. At the end of the year, have the student select three works from his pizza-box portfolio that he would like to have become a part of his permanent portfolio; then you select three additional works. Leave the rest of the student's work inside the pizza-box portfolio. Gift wrap each student's portfolio and add a note that says, "My keepsakes from [number] grade." On the last day of school, deliver each gift-wrapped portfolio to the appropriate student.

Pat Macina—Gr. 2
Southwest Elementary
Howell, MI

Box It Instead

Here's another alternative for portfolio storage. Collect an empty cereal box for each child, and cut off the box top flaps. If desired, spray paint the sides of the box. When the paint is dry, encourage each student to personalize and decorate his box. Once the portfolio boxes are complete, you'll be able to fill each of them with a wider range of things than folders can easily accommodate. For example, consider including an audiotape featuring the student's oral reading, a writing folder or journal, artwork, and anecdotal records.

Tracie Sandin
Frost Lake Elementary
Maplewood, MN

Binder Bonus

Three-ring binders with clear plastic pockets on the front and back covers make especially nice student portfolios. In addition to being sturdy, the binders are easy to decorate. To make a front cover, a student creates a personalized design on a sheet of construction paper (cut to fit the binder pocket), then slips the completed project into the front pocket of his binder. On a second sheet of construction paper, the student glues a snapshot of himself and a paragraph he has written about himself entitled "About The Author." This completed project becomes the back cover of his portfolio.

Throughout the year, select student work for the portfolios. Also ask students to choose their favorite work samples. Date and file all portfolio items in chronological order. At the end of the year, each youngster has a binder that shows his progress over the entire school year.

Lee Nelson—Gr. 2
Rural Point Elementary School
Mechanicsville, VA

Storing Portfolios

This handy filing system makes portfolios easily accessible. Working from an alphabetized list of student names, label and number a hanging file for each student; then insert the files into a hanging file crate in alphabetical/numerical order. Students locate and replace their portfolio files in a snap!

Laurie Howe
Butternut Elementary
North Olmsted, OH

File My Smiles!

Here's a quick and easy way for students to earmark papers they'd like placed in their portfolios. At the beginning of a grading period, give each student a sheet of smiley-face stickers. When a student wants a paper or project filed in his portfolio, he simply attaches a sticker to it; then he returns this work to his teacher or places it in a designated basket. Encourage students to choose a variety of work samples for their portfolios. Periodically replenish your youngsters' allotments of stickers. If desired, change the color of the stickers to coincide with the start of each grading period. Students enjoy earmarking their papers in this manner. And later, when the portfolios are being reviewed, it's easy to tell which papers were student-selected.

Sandra Hoon—Gr. 2, Forest Elementary School, North Olmsted, OH

Portfolios

Journal-Writing Samples

Here's a great way to track students' journal-writing progress. Every Friday, have each student turn to her favorite journal entry of the week. Ask her to be sure the entry is dated; then make a copy of her journal page. Chronologically file each student's duplicated entry in her portfolio. By comparing and contrasting the writing samples in the portfolio, you and the student can evaluate her growth as a writer.

Brenda Cooksey Gee
Mountain View School
Moravian Falls, NC

Handwriting Progress

Monitor the progress of your youngsters' handwriting with this ongoing record. Each month, have the students carefully copy the sentence "This is a sample of my writing" on handwriting paper. Then date the handwriting papers and file them in the students' portfolios. To evaluate a child's writing development, critique his handwriting samples in chronological order. By the year's end, students will be delighted by the visible improvements they see in their handwriting samples.

Nancy Dunaway

Seasonal Illustrations

Here's a great way to track the progression of your youngsters' drawing skills. Each child needs a five-page book of blank drawing paper (four pages plus a cover). Have students label their book covers "[Student's name]'s Drawing Journal." On the first page have students copy and illustrate the sentence "This is how I looked in the fall of [number] grade." When the students' projects are completed, file each student's drawing journal in his portfolio. At the start of the winter season, redistribute the journals. On the next blank page, have students copy and illustrate the sentence "This is how I looked in the winter of [number] grade." Have students illustrate the two remaining seasons in the same manner. To evaluate a youngster's drawing development, simply compare and contrast the four drawings in his completed book.

Nancy Dunaway, Hughes Elementary School, Hughes, AR

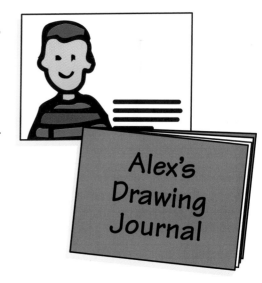

Collecting Work Samples

Sometimes collecting work samples for student portfolios can be challenging—especially if your youngsters are eager to share their best work with their family members. To solve this problem, provide a large resealable plastic bag for each student. Attach a label to each child's bag that includes his name and the message "Portfolio material enclosed! Please return!" If a student wishes to share a paper that has been selected for his portfolio with his family, he slides the paper inside his bag and takes it home. When the paper is returned, it is removed from the bag and filed in the child's portfolio. Now gathering work samples is in the bag!

Laurie Howe, Butternut Elementary, North Olmsted, OH

Portfolio Reviews

Be sure to periodically schedule individual portfolio conferences with your youngsters. During each conference, review the child's portfolio work. Find out which subjects she feels most confident about and which subjects she feels are the most challenging. Encourage the child to set a goal that can be monitored during the next conference time. Also make any appropriate suggestions. For example, if a child is continually choosing art projects as portfolio pieces, urge her to select a greater variety of work. Conclude the conference with several words of praise. If desired, take notes during each conference and file the notations in the child's file for later reference.

Laurie Howe

Student Selections

This nifty tip helps students become part of the evaluation process—an important component of portfolio assessment. In advance, label a file folder for each student; then place all the folders in a portfolio basket. Periodically, samples of each student's work are placed in his portfolio. At the end of each grading period, have each student evaluate his portfolio papers and determine which ones will be graded. Leave the graded papers in the student's portfolio and send the rest home with the student. At the end of the school year, have each student select several graded works that will become a part of his permanent portfolio and allow him to take the remaining graded works home.

Jackie Tinsky—Grs. K–5 Emotionally Handicapped
Bay Crest Elementary, Tampa, FL

Portfolios

Audio Assessments

If you're interested in placing an audiotape in each youngster's portfolio, consider these recording opportunities throughout the grading period. Have each student:

- briefly introduce himself.
- verbalize the things that he does best.
- state his goals for the grading period.
- read a favorite story or chapter of a book.
- tape an oral book report.
- divulge a message for his parent(s).
- confide a message to his teacher.
- describe the events of the day.
- give his opinion on a world event.
- share what's on his mind.

Sandra Hoon—Gr. 2
Teresa Drake—Grs. 2–3
Campton Elementary, Rogers, KY

Opinions Count

Give your students opportunities to voice their opinions about the assignments in their portfolios. Provide copies of the reproducible on page 143. Then encourage each youngster to complete a form to give his feedback on a specific assignment. Periodically remind students that these forms are available for them to use at their discretion.

Kelly A. Wong, Berlyn School, Ontario, CA

Sam B.
Needs practice: "ch"

Carol
Mastered "sl" blend.

New Use for Labels

While observing students at work, you often need to record a comment or note a concern, yet it isn't efficient to pull a student's portfolio each time. Use this easy record-keeping system and your time can be spent with your students—not sifting through files. Keep a sheet of self-stick address labels on a clipboard. Carry the clipboard with you as you observe your students at work. When you see a behavior that requires a note, write it on a label along with the child's name. At the end of the day, transfer each programmed label to the appropriate child's portfolio. This practical record-keeping idea will really stick with you.

Judy Brisbine—Gr. 2
Wessington Springs Elementary
Wessington Springs, SD

Creative-Writing Calendar

Motivate students to write stories that can be used to evaluate progress in creative writing. In advance, make one copy of the calendar on page 144. Program the calendar with the name and dates of the month and fill in each calendar box with a topic for students to write about. Then make a copy of the calendar for each student and staple it to a folder that has been labeled with her name. Each day during the month, have students write about the topic for that particular day. At the end of the month, have each child select three of her creative writings to be placed in her portfolio. Staple the remainder of the writings together and have the student take them home to share with her family. Repeat ther process for each month in the school year. At the end of the year, have the student compare her beginning-of-the-school-year stories to her end-of-the-school-year stories.

Leigh Anne Newsom
Greenbrier Intermediate
Chesapeake, VA

A Portfolio Party

During the last month of school, hold a Portfolio Party to celebrate the progress that your students have made during the school year. To prepare for the celebration, have students write and deliver invitations to their family members. Also have each youngster review her portfolio and select a favorite item that she would like to share with her classmates and the invited guests. Begin the festive affair by giving a motivational speech that describes and reinforces the growth your youngsters have shown. Then have each child take a turn sharing her selected portfolio piece. Finally, serve your student celebrities and their guests cookies and punch. It's a wonderful way to end the school year!

Laura Rosen Horowitz—Gr. 2, Embassy Creek Elementary, Cooper City, FL

Creative-Writing Portfolios

A great place to start using portfolios is with your writing program. If students type the edited versions of their stories into a computer, print two copies of each story. (Or photocopy each student's handwritten version.) Send one copy home with each youngster to share with his family; then date and chronologically file the second copy in the youngster's creative-writing portfolio. By filing stories monthly or biweekly, each child's writing progress is easy to monitor and evaluate.

Doreen Carlo—Gr. 2
Broadview Elementary
Pompano Beach, FL

Matt

Creative Writing

Color-Coded Envelopes

Write each student's name on a 9" x 12" manila envelope. Add a colored piece of construction paper to match the child's reading group and laminate. Children store incomplete center work in their envelopes. They pick up envelopes during free time when they work at centers. When not in use, envelopes are stacked by color.

J. Jacob
Banks Elementary
Baton Rouge, LA

Handyman Bins

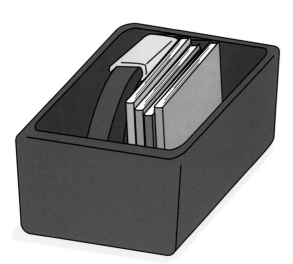

Inexpensive plastic bins are a handy way to organize reading materials. Label one bin for each reading group. Store appropriate student workbooks and teacher's manuals in each bin. Place daily materials, such as duplicated skill sheets, enrichment stories, games, or awards in the appropriate bins as needed. If desired, label one side of each bin for completed student work. The bins are also easy to carry to and from the reading table. This system will be a timesaver for you and a lifesaver for a substitute!

Marilyn Borden—Gr. 3
Castleton Elementary School
Bomoseen, VT

Classroom Checkout

Use this handy pocket system to keep up with the books your students borrow from your class library. Attach a library pocket to the inside cover of each library book. Slip in the pocket a card that you have programmed with the book's title and author. To create a checkout chart, personalize a library pocket for each student and attach the pockets to a sheet of poster board as shown. When a student takes a book from the class library, he removes the card from the book's pocket and places it in his personalized pocket on the checkout chart. When the student is finished with a book, he takes the card from the checkout chart and places it in the book pocket; then he returns the book to the classroom library.

Alice Arksey, Northridge Public School, London, Ontario, Canada

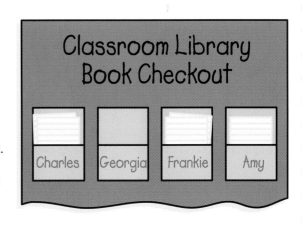

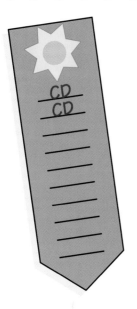

Reading At Home

I ask my students to read aloud to their parents for 15 minutes every night. To help them keep track, I send home a monthly parent letter and bookmark (with a blank for each day of the month). Parents are asked to initial the bookmarks each night after their children read. Completed bookmarks are returned to school at the end of the month to earn small rewards.

Kay Jordan—Gr. 3
Guthrie Elementary School
Memphis, TN

Incentive Bulletin Boards

This activity helps my students stay on task and gives our room an easily decorated bulletin board. Each month, I designate one bulletin board that is to be decorated by students who have completed independent reading work. I choose a holiday theme to which students contribute art. Each student may only add one art piece at a time, and all of his work must be finished first.

Deborah Fay—Gr. 2–3, Fields Road Elementary School, Gaithersburg, MD

Reading Motivator

To motivate children to read, cut a commercially prepared certificate or award (one per student) into six to ten strips. Number the backs of the strips for easy reassembling and place them in individual envelopes labeled with student names. For each student, glue one half of a piece of copy paper to an unusual construction paper shape, label with the student's name, and then mount it on a bulletin board. Each time a student reads a book, glue a strip from his envelope to his shape. Students will enjoy watching their certificates near completion each time they read a book. When each certificate is completed, add an attractive sticker and send the certificate home. This is also a great way to motivate good behavior.

Mary Whaley, Kentland Elementary School, Kentland, IN

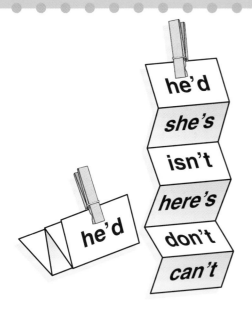

Accordion Lists

For individual skills practice, make lists of special words (such as compounds, contractions, long-vowel) on accordion-pleated papers. Then attach each paper to a bulletin board with a clothespin. The student chooses a list, removes the clothespin, and unfolds the paper to practice skills.

Sr. Ann Claire Rhoads, Mother Seton School, Emmitsburg, MD

Literature Activities

This filing system enables you to keep track of numerous activities designed to accompany a specific children's book you plan to feature. Arrange the titles alphabetically in a storage container. As you encounter an appropriate activity, list the name and page number of the resource on the corresponding card. When you're ready to feature a selected children's book, you'll have a list of activities from which to choose.

Kathleen Darby
Community School
Cumberland, RI

Amelia Bedelia
by Peggy Parish

1991 F/M <u>The Mailbox</u> magazine
Page 55

Who's Next?

To change the pace of who reads next in reading group, use the card system. Make a deck of cards with the names of the children in the reading group plus extra cards such as "read again," "person on your right read," "choose a boy to read," "first girl on your left reads," "teacher's turn," "free choice," etc. Lay the cards facedown in the middle of the reading circle. Pick a child to begin by drawing a card. The child does as the card says. When she is finished reading, she picks the next card.

Jeane Cowin
Elmore Elementary
Elmore, MN

Book Keeping

Keep information about your favorite read-aloud books organized with a personalized card system. On an index card, write the title and author of each book; then note where this book can be found (school library, public library, personal collection) and your students' reactions to it. On the back of the card, list activities that you've done to accompany the story. Put the cards in a recipe box on your desk to keep the information at your fingertips. To remember when you last read the book, pencil the date you complete it on the card.

Renee Sebestyen—Gr. 2
Bayfield Elementary
Durango, CO

The Island of the Skog
by Steven Kellogg
—school library
—children loved it
(12-10-04)

Pairing Partners

Pair students and develop their vocabulary skills with this seasonal approach. Program a class set of seasonal cutouts with pairs of homonyms, antonyms, or synonyms. To assign partners, distribute the shapes and ask each child to find the classmate who holds the homonym (or antonym or synonym) of his word. Once the students are paired, collect and store the cutouts. Your youngsters' vocabulary skills will quickly take shape!

Janice Keer, Irvin Pertzsch School, Onalaska, WI

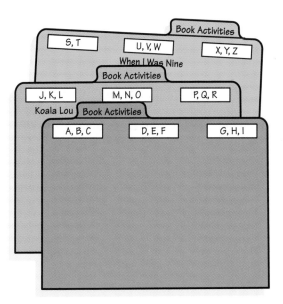

Literature Activity Folders

Organize your literature activities simply and conveniently with three file folders. Label the front of each folder with the letters of the alphabet. (See the illustration.) File each literature activity by the title of the corresponding book; then write the book title on the front of the appropriate folder. Ideas for future literature lessons will be easy to locate.

Melissa Beasley—Chapter I
North Columbia Elementary
Appling, GA

Go "A-head" and Write

Create a quiet environment during independent writing time with an eye-catching hat. When you wear the hat, everyone writes quietly. When you remove the hat, students may ask questions, share their writing with partners, or edit with peers. Now that's using your head!

Shari Abbey—Gr. 3
Abilene Elementary
Valley Center, KS

Proofreading Express

Help students get on the track to good grammar with this activity. Program each page of a spiral chart with three sentences, each of which has grammar, spelling, and punctuation errors. Next to each sentence, write the number of errors contained in the sentence; then display the chart in a convenient classroom location. Each day, turn to a new page and challenge students to locate the errors in the sentences and then copy the sentences correctly into their notebooks. Afterward, enlist students' help in identifying each sentence's errors. Next year, turn back to the first chart page and you're ready to begin again.

Maria Pease—Grs. 2–3 Gifted, Indianapolis Public Schools, Indianapolis, IN

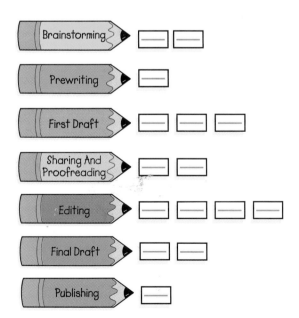

Writers Workshop

Stay informed of where your students are in the writing process with this colorful display. Copy and label seven pencil pattern cutouts (page 69) as shown. Also label a small card for each student. Mount the pencils in sequential order and distribute the student cards. Each child posts her personalized card alongside the pencil that indicates where she is in the writing process. When a student is ready for the next writing stage, she moves her card. A quick glance at the display reveals how the students are progressing and which ones may need assistance during a writers workshop.

Carol Kooken—Gr. 2
Oakbrook School
Wood Dale, IL

A Rainbow of Readers

Most youngsters love to read their creative writings to an audience. There is seldom time, however, for every child to read every day. Here is a great system for helping you ensure that each student will have a chance to read his work aloud by the week's end. When you give a creative-writing assignment, provide five different-colored folders in which students can place their work. Set a limit on the number of papers that can be placed in each folder. Ask students to place their finished work inside one of the folders. Be sure your students understand that if a folder's limit has already been reached, their work must go into a different folder. On each of the next five days, select a different folder and allow the students whose work is inside to read their pieces to you or to the class. After five days have passed, each color will have been chosen.

Brenda Cooksey Gee, Mountain View School, Hays, NC

Problem-Solving Solutions

The next time there's a classroom predicament to solve or a holiday party to plan, enlist your youngsters' problem-solving expertise. Post a brief note that requests your students' advice. In the note, ask that each student submit his ideas to you in the form of a friendly letter. With this simple idea, youngsters have an opportunity to polish their letter-writing skills, share their views, and contribute to classroom solutions!

Jan Keer, Irving Pertzsch Elementary School, Onalaska, WI

"Class-y" Books

Here's a smart way to publish students' writing. Stock a view binder with clear sheet protectors. To make a class book, slip your students' writings into the sheet protectors; then slide a student-decorated cover into the binder's clear pocket. Display the publication in your class library for all to enjoy. In addition to being extremely durable, the class book can be used again and again by simply replacing the students' work.

Joan Hodges—Gr. 2
Lantern Lane Elementary
Houston, TX

Managing Your Lessons

Tracking Student Progress

Keep an up-to-date record of your students' individual progress right at your fingertips! Purchase a flip-top photo album like the one shown. Personalize a card for each student and insert each card in a plastic sleeve. When you wish to make a note about or check on a student's progress, his card is readily available.

Paige Brannon
Pitt County Schools
Greenville, NC

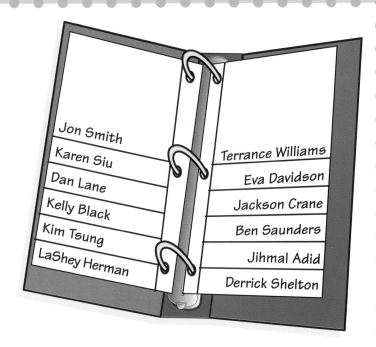

Student Progress Folders

Document student work and keep parents informed with monthly calendars. Staple calendars to the fronts of student work folders. At the end of each day, document student work habits using a code such as the following: C=completed work, I=incomplete work, G=great work. Ask parents to periodically initial the folders. Attach new calendars each month, keeping previous ones for documentation. This method keeps parents up-to-date on their children's accomplishments.

Pam Booth—Gr. 2, H.G. Hill Elementary, Nashville, TN

A =

B =

C =

D =

Pupils' Progress

This color-coded grading system enables you to instantly interpret your students' progress. After recording your youngsters' scores or grades in your grade book, use colored pencils to lightly color over each entry. Use the following code: A=green, B=yellow, C=blue, D or F=red. Then a quick glance at your grade book can give you the information you need.

Sherrel Rudy—Gr. 2
Hoover Elementary
Tulsa, OK

Friendship Fishbowl

Choosing partners or teams for class activities is fun with this fishy procedure. Cut out a supply of construction paper fish patterns (page 142). Personalize one cutout for each student; then place the cutouts in a fishbowl. To create a student group, simply draw the desired number of cutouts from the fishbowl. This method ensures random grouping of youngsters.

Diane Fortunato—Gr. 2
Carteret School
Bloomfield, NJ

Strategy Sticks

Here's a fair and easy way of helping students decide who takes the first turn during small-group and partner settings. Label each of several craft sticks with a different strategy for determining order, such as ABC order by first name, numerical order by birth month and then day, and so on. Keep the sticks in a container on your desk. When an order of play is needed, draw a stick and announce the strategy. Students determine the order in which they take their turns, and then play begins.

Judith Casey—Gr. 3, Milton Avenue School, Chatham, NJ

Picking Partners

Partner cards are perfect for pairing students. To make a set, divide a class supply of blank cards into two equal stacks. Program each card in one stack with a seasonal sticker so that no two cards are the same. Program the second stack of cards to match the first stack. (If you have an uneven number of students, program one wild card.) When it's time for students to pair up, distribute the cards and ask each youngster to quietly find his match. A student with a wild card joins the pair of his choice. Collect and reuse the cards again and again. Easy and fun!

Melanie Cleveland—Gr. 3
Blackduck Elementary
Blackduck, MN

Buddy Sticks

Pair students quickly and save valuable teaching time with buddy sticks. Gather a class supply of craft sticks. Create buddy sticks by applying matching ministickers to the ends of a pair of craft sticks. Make a class supply. Place the buddy sticks in a container so the stickers are not visible. When it's time for students to buddy-up, have each child remove a stick from the container. Then, on a signal from you, students find their partners. Collect the sticks at the completion of the activity. Now that pairing students is such a breeze, your students can have different partners for every activity.

Cheryl Sergi—Gr. 2
Greene Central School
Greene, NY

Creating Teams

Here's a simple way to divide students into teams or groups. To create four teams, you need four different colors of construction paper. From each color, cut the number of three-inch cards that equals one-fourth of your student enrollment. When it's time to play, randomly distribute the cards to your youngsters and ask students to group themselves by color. Four teams will result in a quick, easy, and colorful manner.

Mary Dinneen—Gr. 2, Mountain View School, Bristol, CT

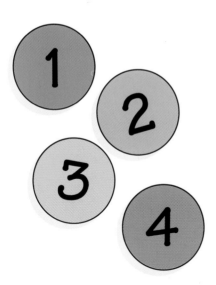

At the Drop of a Circle

Organize your small groups quickly and quietly using this management tip. Assign each group a number; then number a large circle cutout for each group. Laminate the cutouts for durability if desired. When it's time for youngsters to work in their assigned groups, place the circles where you'd like the groups to meet. You'll have a smooth transition into group work and the flexibility to choose the work location that you feel is most appropriate for each group.

Marily Haynos
Scranton, PA

"All Set?" "You Bet!"

Here's a quick way to find out which students are ready for the next task at hand. Simply ask, "All set?" and snap your fingers twice. The students who are ready respond, "You bet!" The others say, "Not yet." If necessary, wait a few moments; then repeat the question. This upbeat exchange prompts students to ready themselves in a timely manner without making them feel anxious.

Maryann Chern Bannwart—Gr. 3
Antietam Elementary
Woodbridge, VA

Now Hear This!

With this idea you can quietly capture the attention of students actively engaged in conversational activities. Simply whisper a direction for students to follow, such as "If you can hear me, touch your ear," or "If you can hear me, raise your hand." As youngsters begin to notice their classmates following your directions, they will tune in to find out what you are saying. Before you know it, your entire class will be all ears.

Beth Bill
Prospect Elementary
Lake Mills, WI

Ready to Begin

Here's an upbeat way to ready students for a new task. During September say, "One apple, two apples, three apples," adjusting the tempo of the phrase to allow sufficient time for students to ready themselves. Then snap your fingers twice, prompting a student response of "Johnny Appleseed!" Count pumpkins in October ("It's harvest time!"), Pilgrims in November ("We are thankful!"), and candles in December ("Happy holidays!"). Timely transitions are guaranteed!

Lynda Wiedenhaupt—Gr., Oshkosh Christian School, Oshkosh, WI

Managing Your Lessons

Random Responses

Keep students tuned in and ready to participate with a customized card deck! Personalize one index card per child and label two more cards "Wild." To use the card deck (for class discussions, large-group reviews, etc.), shuffle it, and then draw cards one by one, calling upon the corresponding students. When a wild card is drawn, the student who answered the previous question answers again or chooses a classmate to answer. Regularly shuffle the deck to keep everyone tuned in! It's a great deal of fun!

Sister Maribeth Theis—Gr. 2
Mary of Lourdes Elementary
Little Falls, MN

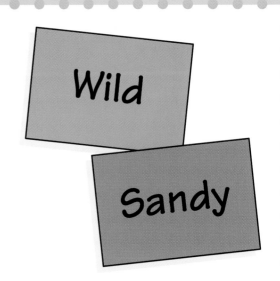

Magic Words

If your students spring into action before you complete oral instructions, consider using magic words. Each morning announce a magic-word category such as cereals or vegetables. Before delivering oral instructions, tell students to remain still and listen carefully until they hear a magic word. After completing your instructions, call a word from the category of the day. Students may follow the given instructions once the word has been called. Keep students on their toes by occasionally calling words from inappropriate categories!

Susan Keith—Gr. 2. Fairview Elementary School, St. Louis, MO

Listening Tip

Hear ye! Hear ye! Use this tip to emphasize information you are delivering. Say to the class, "Give me your left ear!" When students have turned their left ears toward you, share the information. Then say, "Give me your right ear," and restate the information. Last, ask students to repeat the information as you "listen with both ears." Remembering important details like the day field trip permission slips are due and the time the school play starts just got easier for students!

Audrey Gibson—Gr. 3
Ascension Catholic School
Melbourne, FL

Signal System

Cooperative learning is a great teaching strategy, but it can be difficult to monitor each group and determine who needs your help. To check the status of the groups at a glance, give each group a laminated circle that is red on one side and green on the other. When a group is working successfully, it displays the green side of its circle, signaling that the group is on the go with its assignment. When a group needs assistance, it displays the red side of its circle to show that the group has come to a stop. A quick glance around the room will reveal any group that needs your attention.

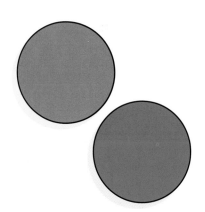

Linda Lovelace—Gr. 3
Halifax Elementary School
Halifax, VA

Conference Waiting Area

When children are involved in the editing and publishing stages of a writing project, it is crucial for them to meet with the teacher several times. To reduce interruptions during individual conferences, set up a conference waiting area. Place four chairs near where student-teacher conferences are held. Students wishing to see the teacher take a seat. If all the seats are full, a student remains at her desk until one of the chairs becomes available. The circle of children waiting for a conference with the teacher will be a thing of the past.

Sandra Lankford—Gr. 2, Lancaster Elementary, Orlando, FL

Assistance Needed

Use this handy display to avoid interruptions while conferencing with individuals or small groups. Have each student trace one of her hands onto tagboard and cut out the resulting shape. Visually divide a display area into multiple sections; then personalize one section for each student. (Sections must be large enough to display hand cutouts.) Attach a Velcro dot to the center of each personalized section; then attach the matching Velcro dot to a hand cutout. Store the cutouts in a basket near the display. When you're busy, a student who needs your assistance attaches a hand cutout to her personalized section. As soon as you're available, glance at the display to see who needs your attention.

Laura Mihalenko—Gr. 2
Truman Elementary School, Parlin, NC

Managing Your Lessons

Watch the Clock

To help children learn the daily schedule and cut down on the incessant "What's next?" draw clock faces on the board with tempera paint. Label each with the activity beginning at that time period. Add the hands daily so you can be flexible. Children watch the clock and match up times to figure out what is coming up. Class changes run as smooth as clockwork.

Sister Margaret Mary, St. Pius Tenth School, Greensboro, NC

Color-Coded Desks

Color-coding your students' desks can save you time in a variety of ways! You will need construction paper circles or sticky dots in four different colors. Arrange your students' desks in groups of four; then attach a different color of circle or dot to each desk in a group. When it's time to distribute materials, call out one of the four colors and you'll have a representative from each group to help you. During group discussions, you can quickly determine a spokesperson for each group by making a color choice. Or use the color code when it's time to tidy the classroom. Just name one of the four colors and ask these students to be the cleanup crew for the day.

Connie Burke—Gr. 3, L. B. J. Elementary, Odessa, TX

Clapping for Quiet

When your students are too noisy, or you just want their attention, clap a rhythm with your hands. The class then imitates the rhythm and waits quietly for another. Repeat rhythms until the whole class is listening. Then give the necessary instructions and they're back to work!

Kristi Pedersen, Barron, WI

Question Marks

To cut down on interruptions when working with a reading or math group, I give each child a laminated index card with a question mark on it. When a child has a question, he puts the card on the top corner of his desk. Between group activities, I go around and answer each question. Often by the time I get to their questions, they have already figured out the answers!

Jane Dickert
Bath Special School
Bath, SC

You Name It!

Enlist your students' help in putting an end to nameless papers. Give each group (or row) of students a paper cup that is to be displayed on a different group member's desk each day. Before an assignment is turned in, the student with the cup on his desk verifies that all papers in his group have names. Each time a group successfully submits only papers with names, place a wooden craft stick in its cup. When a group has earned a designated number of craft sticks, present its members with a special reward or privilege.

Kay A. Fuller—Gr. 2
Clearview Elementary School
Brogue, PA

Nameless Papers

Here's a fun way to remind your students to write their names on their papers. Place an ink pad and a rubber stamp near your turn-in basket. If a child has written his name on his papers, he may stamp his paper before he turns it in. This silent reminder will work wonders!

Linda S. Bowen, Mannford Elementary, Mannford, OK

Reusing Desktags

If changes in your student enrollment make it necessary for you to purchase several sets of desktags each year, try this idea. Laminate a class supply (plus a few extras) of unprogrammed desktags. Then, from clear Con-Tact covering, cut a class supply of strips. Each strip should be approximately one inch longer and wider than a desktag. Use the strips to cover and adhere the desktags to your students' desks. Then, writing atop the clear covering, use a permanent marker to personalize each desktag. When a student moves away, peel away the strip of programmed covering. You'll be left with a good-as-new desktag that can be used again and again!

Marie Lain
Marjory Stoneman Douglas Elementary
Miami, FL

ADAM

Welcome Book

First-day introductions will be a snap with this letter-perfect class book! Have each youngster write a letter to the anticipated student teacher, leaving space for an illustration or a photograph of himself. Encourage each student to include information in his letter about his family, friends, interests, and/or favorite subjects. After each child has taped to his letter a photo of himself (or drawn and colored a self-portrait), bind the completed projects and a welcome letter from you between student-decorated covers. Surprise your student teacher with this special keepsake on her first day. The intern will no doubt appreciate (and enjoy!) this directory of student information!

Debbie Fly—Gr. 3, Edgewood School, Homewood, AL

Welcome-Book Variation

For a high-tech variation of the welcome-book project on this page, have each student type his letter using a word-processing program such as ClarisWorks. Take his picture with a digital camera; then insert the picture into his letter.

LeAnn Knoeck—Grs. K–5 Learning Disabilities
Taft Elementary, Neenah, WI

"Hand-y" Tote Bag

This welcome gift is sure to be a hands-down favorite! First, decorate a plain canvas tote bag. To do this, apply fabric paint to each student's palm and have her carefully make her handprint on the bag. Then have each student use a fabric marker to sign her name near her handprint. Fill the decorated bag with a variety of teaching goodies—such as a lesson-plan book, stickers, decorative notepads, and grading pens—and then present the bag to your student teacher. No doubt she will appreciate the convenience of having these materials on hand!

Kelly A. Lu—Gr. 2
Berlyn School
Ontario, CA

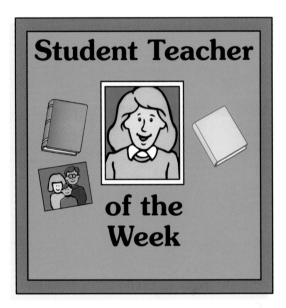

Student Teacher of the Week

What better way to acquaint youngsters with the student teacher than by featuring her as student teacher of the week? With your students' permission, take a week off from your existing student-of-the-week program to feature your intern. During her first week, ask the newcomer to bring to school a few items, such as family photos and favorite books. Using your established student-of-the-week format or a modified version, have the student teacher share and display these special items. With this ice-breaking activity, youngsters will soon feel at ease with your intern. Plus she will feel honored to have had a turn in the spotlight!

Julie Davenport, W. A. Wright Elementary, Mt. Juliet, TN

Scheduling Savvy

Looking for a way to communicate the responsibilities your intern can expect? Try this weekly timetable! With your student teacher's input, establish a weekly schedule that outlines her duties during the practicum. Then make a copy of the schedule for the student teacher and file the original for future reference. With this plan, your intern will know what to anticipate and she can prepare accordingly!

Lu Brunnemer
Eagle Creek Elementary
Indianapolis, IN

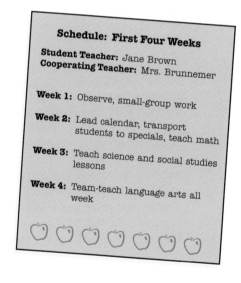

Schedule: First Four Weeks

Student Teacher: Jane Brown
Cooperating Teacher: Mrs. Brunnemer

Week 1: Observe, small-group work

Week 2: Lead calendar, transport students to specials, teach math

Week 3: Teach science and social studies lessons

Week 4: Team-teach language arts all week

Please place an extra copy _____

An Extra Special Gift

Extra reproducibles can add up to a fantastic student-teacher gift! Decorate and label a large box with your student teacher's name. Then place the box in the teachers' workroom near the copier. Post a note asking each teacher to place in the box an extra copy of each item she duplicates. (Also request that the teacher write her name and/or room number on the back of each copy.) Give the student teacher this box of reproducibles during the last week of her practicum. If she has a question about any page, she can ask the teacher who donated it. Now that's a simple and inexpensive way to gather a large assortment of teaching materials!

Maryann Chern Bannwart—Gr. 3, Antietam Elementary, Woodbridge, VA

Student Teacher

Home, Sweet Home

Here's a thoughtful idea that will make your student teacher feel right at home! Designate a desk (or table) for his use only and stock it with a decorative teacher's mug; a pencil cup; and a basket full of school supplies, such as scissors, tape, glue, chalk, and pens. Be sure to add a nametag to the desk too. Your student teacher will appreciate having his own space and teaching supplies!

Teresa A. DeMatties—Gr. 2
Walberta Park School
Syracuse, NY

Valuable Viewpoints

Use a two-step feedback process to establish clear communication with your student teacher. Each day as your student teacher conducts a lesson, record your observation notes in two columns labeled as follows: "What Went Well" and "Suggestions for Future Lessons." After the lesson, have the student teacher reflect upon the teaching experience and note her thoughts in these areas: "What Went Well," "Things I'd Like to Change," and "Goals." At the end of the day, meet with the student teacher and compare your observations with her notes. Focus on positive aspects of the observed lesson; then discuss her goals and possible strategies for reaching them. Lastly, photocopy your observations and her notes so that each of you can file one set for future reference. This ongoing feedback will be a priceless part of the student-teaching experience!

Teresa DeMatties—Gr. 2

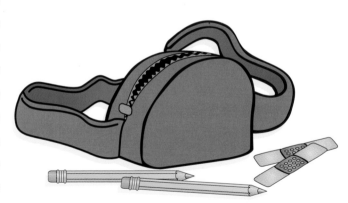

Pack Up for Recess!

It's important to be prepared when duty calls—recess duty, that is! Give your student teacher a helping hand by assembling a recess supply kit for her. Fill a fanny pack with important items, such as first aid supplies, office passes, and a pencil. Then use a length of cord or heavy string to attach a whistle to the zipper pull. Your student teacher will be packed up and ready for recess in a jiffy!

Betsy Crosson—Gr. 2
Pleasant School
Tulare, CA

Farewell Flower

Thankful thoughts and good wishes will bloom with this "plant-astic" goodbye gift! On the rim of a clay flowerpot, use a paint pen or permanent marker to write your student teacher's name. Then have each youngster sign his name on the pot with a colorful permanent marker. Be sure to add your signature too. Transplant a small flower or other greenery into the signed pot, and present this unique memento to the student teacher on her last day.

Lana Stewart—Gr. 2
Wills Point Primary School
Wills Point, TX

Keepsake Notebook

Keep this class project top secret—until your student teacher's last day, that is! Without your intern's knowledge, have each student describe and illustrate a special memory of his time with the student teacher. Place each student's completed page in a three-ring binder and slip a class photo in the binder's cover. Add a title page and a goodbye message that has been autographed by students. Your student teacher will cherish this notebook of memories!

Kathi Delp—Gr. 2
Paterson Elementary
Orange Park, FL

Fall Quarter

9/10 Emily ∿∿∿∿∿∿
∿∿∿∿∿∿∿∿∿∿∿

Doable Documentation

Take a practical approach to documenting student behavior. Write each child's name on a Post-it index flag. Attach each flag to a different page of a spiral notebook, leaving four blank pages between flags. Program each flagged page with family and medical information about the named student. Label each set of blank pages for the four quarters of the school year. To document student behavior, simply turn to the appropriate notebook page and then date and note your observation. Now that's doable!

Irene Thayer
Odebolt-Arthur Community School
Odebolt, IA

Here's the Homework

There's no denying the importance of being well rested and well fed before testing begins. Here's one way to make sure that your youngsters' parents are aware of these important elements as well. As the only homework for the evening, send home a two-item checklist for parents to sign. The two assignments are "Go to bed early" and "Eat a good breakfast." With no other homework to distract them, youngsters may be more likely to take care of these essentials.

Keys to Success

Cast away your youngsters' test-taking doubts with personalized keys to success. Personalize one construction paper key for each student; then flip the cutouts over and write "Success" on the blank sides. If desired, laminate the keys for durability. Then punch a hole in each key and create a necklace by threading a length of yarn or ribbon through the hole. On the day that testing is to begin, adorn each youngster with his key to success. Encourage students to wear their keys during each testing session.

Success

Alex

Taking a Break

There's an inherently relaxing quality about kneading and molding play dough. So during testing breaks, consider giving each youngster a small snack and a portion of homemade dough.

To prepare the play dough, mix one cup of flour, one-half cup of salt, and two teaspoons of cream of tartar in a saucepan. Stir in one cup of water, one tablespoon of cooking oil, and five drops of food coloring. Cook this mixture over low heat for three minutes or until it makes a soft ball of dough. Then remove the dough from the heat and knead it until smooth. Separate the dough into individual portions; then store the portions in Ziploc bags until it's time for a testing break.

The Time Element

One facet of the testing situation that can make your youngsters uncomfortable is the time restriction. Several weeks prior to testing, begin to minimize this stress by having children complete review work within a specified time limit. At the conclusion of each of these timed reviews, give youngsters a test-taking hint related to their anxieties. For example, discuss that it's a good idea to complete all of the "easy" problems first and come back to the more difficult ones. This is also an excellent opportunity to discuss how quickly time slips away when one is concentrating on a specific task.

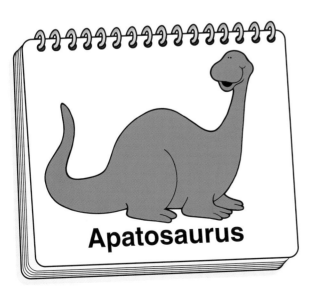

Apatosaurus

Just for the Fun of It!

Give your youngsters something to look forward to during testing week. Find out what their favorite theme is. (For many youngsters the favorite topic is dinosaurs.) After testing is concluded each day, involve youngsters in fun learning experiences related to this popular theme. The children appreciate this break from the usual routine. And, since a lot of fun coincides with testing week, you'll probably notice a positive change in their spirit!

Fish Patterns

Use with "Friendship Fishbowl" on page 129.

Name: _____

Date: _____ Assignment: _____

This assignment was Easy   Hard
(Color one box.)
☐ ☐ ☐ ☐ ☐ ☐ ☐ ☐ ☐ ☐ ☐ ☐ ☐ ☐

If I could do this assignment over, I would _____

_____ .

The best part of this assignment was _____

_____ .

One thing I learned from this assignment was _____

_____ .

©The Education Center, Inc. • *500 Classroom Tips* • TEC60848

Name: _____

Date: _____ Assignment: _____

This assignment was Easy   Hard
(Color one box.)
☐ ☐ ☐ ☐ ☐ ☐ ☐ ☐ ☐ ☐ ☐ ☐ ☐ ☐

If I could do this assignment over, I would _____

_____ .

The best part of this assignment was _____

_____ .

One thing I learned from this assignment was _____

_____ .

©The Education Center, Inc. • *500 Classroom Tips* • TEC60848

Name _____

My creative-writing calendar for _____

Monday	Tuesday	Wednesday	Thursday	Friday

144

Note to the teacher: Use with "Creative-Writing Calendar" on page 121.

Student Motivation and Work Management

Contents

Good Behavior

Rules for Good Listeners

Here's an easy way to remind students to be good listeners. Post a chart that lists rules for good listening. When a student needs to be reminded of a particular rule, point to the rule on the chart. This silent reminder helps the student remember the rule without interrupting the lesson.

Vini Hodge
Bergman, AR

Rules for Good Listening
- are still.
- are quiet.
- are silent.
- are watching.
- are listening.

Behavioral Contract

This year ask your students to help you write your list of school rules. With student input, list desirable behaviors in a positive way. For example, list "Walk quietly in the hallway." Record the list of rules in contract form on a large sheet of poster board. Have each student sign his name at the bottom before displaying the contract in your classroom.

Teri Butson
John Price School
Lancaster, PA

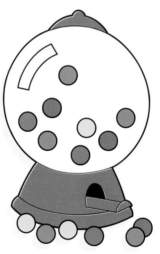

Bubble Gum Club

For a motivating bulletin board, I make a cut-out bubble gum machine for each child. Each day that a student finishes his work, he puts a circle sticker on his machine. At the end of the week, we count the stickers. Whoever has the most gumballs gets a penny to buy a piece of gum from our class gumball machine.

Jana Jensen
Gillette, WY

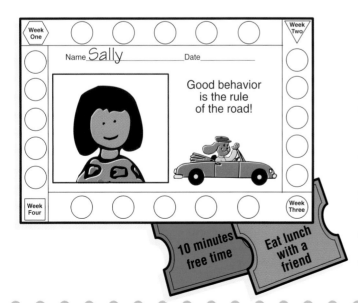

Name Sally   Date _____

Good behavior is the rule of the road!

Week One Week Two Week Three Week Four

10 minutes free time

Eat lunch with a friend

Driver's License

Your students will be zooming towards good behavior with this behavior-modification approach. Duplicate a driver's license pattern (page 177) for each student; then have her fill in her name and the date, and color a self-portrait in the box. Discuss the importance of staying parked in your garage (desk), muffling your motor (voice), and driving on your side of the highway (hallway). At the end of each week, reward each student who has not had her license punched for a negative behavior by presenting her with a programmed coupon pattern from page 177). Begin each month with new licenses. Good behavior will be the rule of the road!

Viola Gardner
Bertrand, NE

Graph a Treat

Try this graphic approach to positive reinforcement. On 1-inch-square graph paper, draw an outline for each of the following letters: T, R, E, A, T. Display the resulting sign in a prominent location. Each time your class displays a desired behavior (such as working quietly or carefully following directions), use a marker to color an enclosed area inside one letter. When the letters are completely colored, celebrate by rewarding class members with special treats.

Susan Grimm—Gr. 3
Lukeville Elementary
Brusly, LA

Warm-Fuzzy Jar

Encourage your students to work quietly and re-member their manners with a warm-fuzzy jar. Simply place a cotton ball in a pint canning jar each time a positive behavior is displayed. A full jar of warm fuzzies earns an extra class recess.

Teri Butson
Lancaster, PA

Super Kids Box

At the beginning of the day, I draw a box on the chalk-board labeled "Super Kids." (I sometimes label the box "Super Santas," "Super Bunnies," or another seasonal title.) When a child is caught doing a good deed, he gets to write his name in colored chalk in the box. If he contin-ues to follow class rules, his name stays up for the rest of the day. At the end of the day, he may choose one of our classroom awards. Students love writing their names on the board and work hard to receive the awards.

Randi Fields—Gr. 2
Tampa, FL

Good Behavior

A Motivational Punch

Motivate your students to complete tasks on time using teacher-made punch cards. Distribute small tagboard cards labeled with student names. Punch student cards for tasks completed on time. Upon reaching predetermined point values, students cash in their punched cards for rewards (stickers, bookmarks) or privileges (line leader, free time).

Sharon Stack
Pine Tree Elementary
Longview, TX

Good Behavior Marbles

When a student exhibits good behavior, call out that child's name and drop a marble in a jar on your desk. The sound of the marble dropping reminds the rest of the students to do their best. Add an extra incentive by holding a popcorn party when the jar is full.

Gail Felker
Park City, IL

Red Carpet Kids

Each day I select a student to be the Red Carpet Kid for the day, based on classroom and playground behavior. The Red Carpet Kid gets special attention on his day and sits on a red carpet square placed on his seat. I keep a record of the Kids to make sure everyone has a turn once every month.

Dianne Labor
Pinedale Elementary School
Rapid City, SD

Assertive Discipline Bonus

Pair this class incentive with your current Assertive Discipline plan. Determine a reward such as a candy, an ice-cream, or a popcorn treat that students can earn by displaying positive group behaviors. Write each letter needed to spell the reward on a separate sheet of construction paper. Display the sheets facedown in a prominent place. When students successfully display positive behaviors throughout the day, flip over one concealed letter. When all the letters are displayed, present students with their earned reward. Choose a new incentive and begin the process again. Students will strive for good behavior when the reward is clearly in sight.

Jean M. Rosemeyer
Abbotsford, WI

Tickets Galore!

Here's the winning ticket for easy classroom management! Award a commercially printed tickets or a copy of the pattern on page 177 to each student who is on task or displaying appropriate behavior. Have each recipient write his name on his ticket(s). Then, at the end of the day, have students place their tickets in a jar. Each Friday, draw several tickets from the jar and present each lucky winner with a special treat.

Pamela Myhowich—Gr. 2, Dick Scobee Elementary School, Auburn, WA

Blossoming Behavior

Positive classroom behaviors will blossom using these beautiful incentive baskets. Have each student attach a basket cutout to a sheet of construction paper as shown. Cut a supply of flower shapes from wallpaper and gift wrap. When a student displays positive behaviors throughout the day, reward him with a flower cutout to glue atop his construction paper basket. When his basket is filled with a predetermined number of beautiful blossoms, present the student with a small reward and a new basket cutout to fill.

Wanda R. Reding

Gotcha!

Keep your youngsters quietly working on task with a supply of Gotcha awards. Periodically survey the room with the intention of awarding these reproducible awards (see page 178); then give an award to each student that you catch quietly working on a task. At the end of each day, have students sign the backs of the awards and deposit them in a designated container. Each week draw one award from the box and present the child with a special prize or privilege. Return the remaining awards to the appropriate students.

Susan Underwood
Hockanum School
East Hartford, CT

End-of-Year Auction

Clean out your closets and motivate your students with a June auction. Students accumulate points in class to spend at the auction. Give points for doing class chores, finishing extra work, completing centers, etc. Keep track of these points. In June, give each child a card showing his or her total points. Clean out your cupboards for old magazines, plants, games, lost and found items, etc. Auction each of these off to the highest bidder, deducting that number of points on the child's card as an item is purchased. Include a mystery item—such as a snakeskin in a paper bag—for added excitement.

Teresa Wilkinson, Hope, B.C., Canada

Party Plan

Encourage your students to display super behavior outside the classroom. Make and laminate 18 popcorn cutouts. Each time your students leave the classroom, a popcorn cutout is given to the teacher in charge. If the entire class behaves, the cutout is returned with the students and placed in a bowl in the classroom. When the bowl is full, have a popcorn party! For the next party plan, try cookie or ice cream cut outs.

Marlene Schriefer
Halliday School
Halliday, ND

Terrific News!

Preprogramming positive notes with your students' names eliminates time-consuming record keeping. Make a class supply of the "Terrific News" notes on page 179 and personalize one for each student. Each day acknowledge three well-behaved students by jotting each a positive note. Before your class leaves for the day, present the "Terrific News" notes to the deserving students. When you run out of personalized notes, you'll know that each child has received a positive note during the past few weeks. Then make and personalize another class set of notes and you can begin the process again!

Lu Brunnemer
Eagle Creek Elementary
Indianapolis, IN

Weekly Updates

Weekly correspondence with your students' parents is so important, yet it can be very time-consuming. Use this weekly checklist to economize your time. Personalize a folder for each student. Fill in the grading codes on the weekly report form (page 179) with your own symbols; then staple a copy of the report inside each child's folder. During the week, file corrected papers in the folders. On Friday, complete each child's checklist; then send each child's folder home with him. Ask students to return their folders and initialed checklists to school on Monday. (Students' papers remain at home.) If desired, present a small reward, such as a sticker, to each student who returns his folder on time.

Susan Barnett—Gr. 3, Northwest Elementary, Ft. Wayne, IN

Weekly Reports

Keep parents updated on classroom happenings with these weekly reports. Each Friday, make a copy of page 180. Fill in the dates and program the lower portion of the report iwth information for the upcoming week. Next, make student copies. Label and complete one report (based on the past week's behavior) for each student. At the end of the day, send home the reports. A parent signs the report and then detaches and retains the lower portion. The child returns the signed portion to school the following Monday.

Donna Ransdell—Substitute Teacher
Cajon Valley Union School District
El Cajon, CA

Good Behavior

Spotting Good Behavior

Looking for a colorful way to reinforce positive classroom behavior? This idea really hits the spot! Arrange student desks into groups of four or five. Assign each group of students a different color. Label one manila envelope for each group and display the envelopes on a bulletin board or chalk ledge. Also cut out a supply of round construction paper circles (spots) in each designated color. Each time you observe a group exhibiting outstanding classroom behavior, slip a colored spot in its envelope. At the end of the week, let each group count the spots it earned.

If desired, reward each group that earns a predetermined number of spots for the week with a special privilege or small individual prizes.

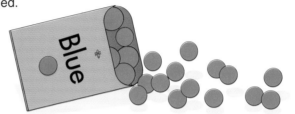

Candi Barwinski—Gr. 2
Fleetwood Elementary School
Fleetwood, PA

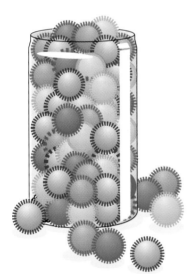

Collecting Class Compliments

Reinforce positive student behavior with this one-of-a-kind idea. All you need is a clean, empty container and a supply of pom-poms. Each time the class receives a compliment from you or another staff member, drop a pom-pom into the container. When the container is half-full, present each student with a sticker or another small reward; when it's completely filled, plan a class party. You can count on this incentive to keep end-of-the-year behavior in line!

Gina Marinelli—Gr. 2, B. Bernice Young Elementary School, Burlington, NJ

Compliment Chain

Recognize and reward your students' outstanding behavior with a compliment chain. Keep a supply of construction paper strips handy. Each time your class receives a behavior-related compliment from a staff member, parent volunteer, or other adult, add a link to the chain. When a predetermined number of links is earned, reward students with a popcorn party or another desired treat or privilege.

Jennifer Norman
Maplewood Elementary
Ocala, FL

Sweet Comments

These lovely lollipops encourage students to recognize their class-mates' positive qualities. To make his lollipop, a student personalizes and decorates a four-inch construction paper circle; then he glues the circle near the top of a tongue depressor. Store the lollipops in a plastic jar. Each week gather students in a circle and distribute the lol-lipops, making sure no child receives his own. Ask each child, in turn, to share with the class something he especially likes about the class-mate whose lollipop he is holding. Then collect the lollipops and store them until the following week!

Denise Mason
Port Reading School
Port Reading, NJ

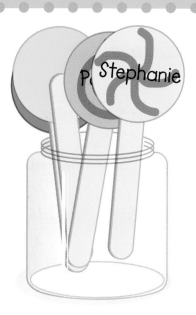

Marvelous Manners

Promote good manners with a marvelous manners box. Decorate a box with colorful paper; then program the outside of the box with an assortment of polite phrases such as "Thank you," "You are very welcome," "Excuse me," and "Please let me help you." Next to the box, place a supply of manner tickets (blank paper slips). Each time you observe a student demonstrating marvelous manners, in-vite the child to sign a manners ticket and deposit it in the marvelous manners box. Every Friday draw a ticket from the box. Present the winning student with a privilege or a small prize.

Jennifer Ursta—Gr. 2, Claude Huyck School, Kansas City, KS

Compliments Chain

To increase your students' good behavior and build their self-esteem, try this positive approach to discipline. Copy the poem below onto a desired tagboard shape; then use an X-acto knife to slit the lower edge of the cutout. (The slit should be approximately two inches in length.) To start your chain of compliments, insert a construction paper strip through the slit; then glue the ends of the strip together. Prominently suspend the resulting poster from your classroom ceiling. Each time your students receive a compliment from a member of the school staff, a parent volunteer, or another visiting adult, attach a link to the chain. When the chain reaches the floor, reward your stu-dents as desired.

Peggy Smith
Skyland Elementary
Lyman, SC

> For all the nice things people say,
> We'll add another link today.
> And when the chain and floor do meet,
> Mrs. Smith will bring us a treat.

Good Behavior

A Great Lunch Bunch!

Harvest a bunch of positive lunchroom behavior with this incentive plan! Display a paper grape stem with the title "What a Great Bunch!" Each time the class receives a good report from lunchroom monitors, add a paper grape to the display. When a predetermined number of grapes is earned, reward your bunch with a raisin treat!

Lisa Olson
Maplewood Elementary
Coral Springs, FL

Links for Lining Up

Motivate students to line up quickly and quietly with this paper-chain incentive. Keep a supply of construction paper strips and a stapler on hand. To begin, tape one link of a paper chain to the top of the door frame. Explain to your students that each time they line up satisfactorily, they will earn an additional link on the chain. When the paper chain extends to a predetermined length, reward the students with a special treat or privilege. Continue offering added incentives as the length of the chain increases.

Jennifer Ursta & Sandra Loudon—Gr. 2, Claude Huyck School, Kansas City, KS

Lunchroom Behavior

Reduce behavior problems in the lunchroom with this positive plan. Personalize a clothespin for each child and then display the clothespins so they are easy for students to retrieve. As each child lines up for lunch he collects his clothespin and clips it to his shirt sleeve. If he returns to the classroom (after lunch) with his clothespin in place, he earns one point for the class. If he is involved in a behavior-related incident and asked to surrender his clothespin, he earns no point. When a set number of class points are earned, reward the class with extra recess time!

Jennifer Norman
Maplewood Elementary
Sunrise, FL

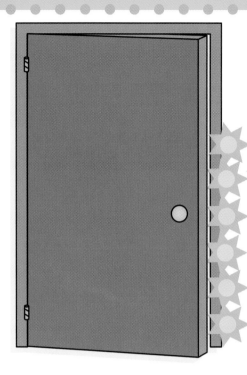

Timely Arrivals

This positive approach sends a clear message about the importance of punctuality! For every morning that all students arrive on time, tape a seasonal cutout to the door frame. Begin where the frame and floor connect, and then continue taping cutouts around the frame. When the entire door frame is covered, reward the class with a special treat and an extra privilege.

Linda C. Harris—Gr. 2
Dobbs Elementary
Rockwall, TX

Low-Key Lights

Encourage students to leave high-spirited recess behavior on the playground! Display indoor holiday lights around the perimeter of a chalkboard or bulletin board. Before recess ends, plug in the holiday lights and turn off the overhead lights. When students step into the tranquil environment, they quickly calm down!

Margie Siegel—Gr. 2, Wren Hollow Elementary School, Ballwin, MO

Class Pet

A snuggly stuffed animal is a great tool to encourage positive classroom behavior. Introduce your children to their new class pet and allow the children to give the pet a name. Throughout the day, look for students who are following directions, staying on task, or demonstrating positive behavior. Reward those children by placing the stuffed animal on their desks for designated periods of time.

Mary Dinneen—Gr. 2
Mountain View School
Bristol, CT

Good Behavior

Hallway Behavior

Promote positive hallway behavior with this management tip. First, have each student identify a person that she admires. Explain that whenever the students are walking in the hallway, you would like them to imagine that these people are walking right beside them. Discuss the types of behavior that would make these imaginary partners feel proud. Then periodically invite students to tell how these companions have influenced their hallway behavior. For added motivation, have students choose new imaginary partners from time to time.

Anne Esau Ballard—Gr. 2
West Homestead Elementary
Homestead, FL

Hallway Management

An imaginary high wire may prove successful in transporting students quickly and quietly through school hallways. When traveling from one location to another, have students pretend they are tightrope walkers. Whether the students are following a line in the linoleum or an imaginary high wire, their intense concentration makes for a surprisingly quiet hallway journey!

Brooke A. Bock—Gr. 2, Warriors Mark Elementary, Tyrone, PA

Spotting Good Behavior

Help your youngsters stretch toward perfect hallway behavior with this fun-filled idea. Cut out a tall giraffe shape from yellow paper and 20 giraffe spots from brown paper. Add facial features and other desired details to the giraffe; then laminate the cutout and the spots. Display the giraffe in an accessible classroom area and store the spots nearby. Each time the class shows exceptional hallway behavior, have a student tape a spot on the giraffe. Reward the class with a special treat or privilege when all 20 spots are in place. What a gigantic way to encourage positive hallway behavior!

Leann Schwartz—Gr. 2
Ossian Elementary School
Ossian, IN

Touchdown!

Score big with this super incentive plan. Program a length of green bulletin board paper to resemble a football field. Help each student set several achievable goals for himself; then have him write each goal on a strip of paper. Have the student select one goal to strive for and tape the matching strip to his desk, and then tuck the remaining strips inside a personalized envelope. Later have each student evaluate his success. Personalize a football sticker for each student who achieved his goal; then, starting at the left end zone, place the stickers end to end on the field. Then have students select new goals from their envelopes and tape them to their desks. When the stickers reach the opposite end zone, reward the entire class with a special treat. It's a touchdown!

Janice Ford, Pinewood Park Elementary, Gilmer, TX

Good Behavior Bulletin Board

Ahoy, mateys! Here's the key to great student behavior! Program a paper strip with the title "The Key to the Treasure Is Good Behavior!"; then staple the paper near the top of a bulletin board. Use a pushpin to suspend a key cutout below the first letter in the title. Staple a decorated treasure chest cutout to the right of the paper strip. Tuck a small card labeled with a class reward or privilege behind the treasure chest. Each time that the class exhibits exemplary behavior throughout the day, move the key to the right one letter. Continue in this manner until the key reaches the treasure chest. Then remove the card and reveal what treasure the students have earned. No doubt your youngsters will do their best to be as good as gold!

Fran Rizzo—Gr. 3, Brookdale School, Bloomfield, NJ

Party on Pluto

This out-of-sight motivational plan encourages stellar student behavior! On a bulletin board covered with dark colored paper, mount cutouts of the sun and each of the nine planets. Use a pushpin to attach a spaceship cutout to the sun. Then mount a trail of star cutouts that begins at the sun, ends on Pluto, and connects all the planets in between. Each time the class demonstrates terrific behavior, move the spaceship forward one star. If the spaceship lands on a planet, reward the class with a special privilege such as five minutes of extra recess. When the spaceship lands on Pluto, treat your youngsters to a well-deserved stellar celebration! Far-out!

Jennifer Ellis—Gr. 3
Tom Green Elementary
Buda, TX

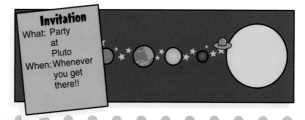

Good Behavior

"Tape" Five!

When a petty dispute arises between students, this approach encourages the youngsters to work out their problem independently. Instruct the students who are involved in the dispute to go to a classroom area where a tape recorder has been set up. Then have the children turn the tape recorder on and talk out their problem. Provide a timer to make sure the students stay within a five-minute time limit. Later in the day, after the students have had a chance to cool off, sit with the youngsters as they listen to their recording. By this time students often realize just how silly their argument was.

Sr. Barbara Flynn
St. Raphael School
Bridgeport, CT

Private Time

Promote positive student behavior by creating a space in your classroom where youngsters can voluntarily spend a few minutes alone. A chair or a large pillow placed in a classroom nook is all you'll need. Encourage students to visit the area when they need a few minutes to sort through their thoughts and feelings. This unique approach teaches students a positive method for dealing with their emotions, builds self-esteem, and endorses exemplary behavior.

Tina Robertson, Kensington Road School, Glens Falls, NY

Thumbs-Up Behavior

Promote positive classroom behavior with this easy-to-maintain display! Mount the title "Thumbs Up for Good Behavior" and prepare a colorful supply of cutouts like the one shown. At the end of each day, quickly review the class's behavior. When it is satisfactory, add a cutout to the display. If an improvement is needed, provide a behavior pointer. When a predetermined number of cutouts are posted, reward the class with a special treat or privilege. Then remove the posted cutouts and repeat the positive plan!

Lee Rodrigue
Vacherie Primary
Vacherie, LA

Colorful Reminders

Colorful apple cutouts are just what you need to monitor classroom noise. Post a red apple to signal a quiet work time. Post a yellow apple when a moderate level of noise is acceptable. If any noise level is OK, post a green apple. Students respond to the colorful cues and that means you'll receive a bushel of cooperation!

Janica Peppard
Pine Tree Academy
Freeport, ME

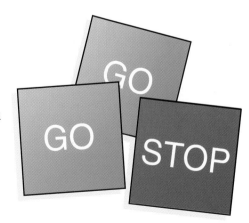

Voice Meter

When your entire class is engaged in hands-on activities, a certain level of noise is anticipated. Keeping the noise level in check can be challenging. This idea helps your students monitor their own noise level. On the chalkboard draw a voice meter similar to the one shown. Explain to your students that each time the noise level in the classroom becomes too loud, you will color in a portion of the meter. If the meter reaches the top, it will be necessary for you to stop the activity. This method places the responsibility of noise control on the students themselves and keeps them aware of the consequences of their actions. Now, instead of using your voice to talk above the noise, you can use it to praise your youngsters' great behavior.

Christine M. Belvin—Grs. K–3, Public School 153, Bronx, NY

Behavior Plan

Use this plan to keep classroom behavior on course! When the class exhibits outstanding behavior, drop green paper GO squares into a designated container. When inappropriate behavior occurs, deposit red paper STOP squares. At the end of each day, remove a square from the container. A green GO square earns the class ten minutes of free time! Repeat the activity each day, always starting the day with an empty container.

Renee Kerstetter—Gr. 3
Selinsgrove Area Intermediate School
Selinsgrove, PA

Good Behavior Tickets

Ticketing your youngsters' good behavior paves the way to a positive classroom environment! Use rubber stamps to decorate a supply of 1" x 2" blank paper tickets. Hand out the tickets in acknowledgement of your youngsters' positive behaviors. When a student collects ten tickets, she redeems them for a small prize or a special privilege.

Christy Martin—Gr. 2
Weddington Elementary
Matthews, NC

Weekly Homework Bonus

Here's the ticket to completed student homework! Schedule a lunchtime video every Friday. Invite each child who successfully completes her homework for the week to view the video. If students routinely eat their lunches in the classroom, arrange for a parent volunteer to show the video in another food-friendly school location.

Ashley Rebman—Substitute Teacher, Durham, NC

Good Behavior Bonus

An element of chance adds to the appeal of this weekly behavior reward! Survey students to discover the kinds of rewards they find most appealing. Then write several suggested rewards (like "ten minutes of extra recess" or "watch a book-related video") on individual paper slips. Place the strips in a gift bag. Tell the class that each Friday every student who displayed outstanding classroom behavior throughout the week earns a good behavior bonus. Explain that the bonus will be drawn from the bag of student-suggested rewards on Thursday afternoon (giving you time to prepare) and presented on Friday afternoon. Outstanding classroom behavior is in the bag!

Linnae Nicholas—Gr. 2
Cuba Elementary School
Cuba, NY

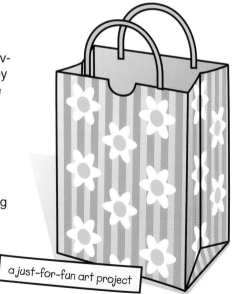

a just-for-fun art project

Sunshine Basket

Show students that their good behavior brightens your day! Place a small basket within easy student reach. Each time you observe a student displaying exemplary behavior, ask her to personalize a small sun cutout and then drop it in the basket. At the end of each week, draw several names from the basket and reward each of these students with a small treat or happy note. Then empty the basket and you're ready to reinforce positive behavior the following week. Let the sun shine in!

Gina Marinelli—Gr. 2
Bernice Young Elementary
Burlington, NJ

Points for Positive Behavior

Reinforce positive classroom behavior with this reward system. Enlist your students' help in determining the number of class points that can be earned when the majority of the group displays specific positive behaviors. For example, walking quietly in the hallway might be worth five points and working cooperatively in the classroom worth ten points. If desired, designate points for behaviors that require total class participation, such as perfect attendance. Next, set up a point-keeping system and determine the total number of points the class must earn in order to receive an agreed-upon reward. With this system in place, everyone can celebrate the rewards of positive behavior!

Vida Vaitkus—Gr. 3, Marvin School, Norwalk, CT

Behavior Incentive

Encourage positive student behavior with an easy-to-manage incentive. Think of an incentive in the form of a sentence, such as "An extra recess sure would be nice!" Then, on the chalkboard, draw a series of blanks to represent each word in the sentence—one blank per letter. Each time you observe students exhibiting a positive classroom behavior, write a letter in one blank. When all the blanks are filled and the incentive is revealed, reward the students accordingly. You can count on students trying to guess the class reward as they practice positive classroom behaviors!

Sandy Wiele—Gr. 2
Peoria Christian School
Peoria, IL

Good Behavior

Praising With Popcorn

Promote class cooperation by sponsoring a popcorn party. You will need a bag of unpopped popcorn, a small scoop, and a large transparent container. Each time you notice students working well together, place a scoop of popcorn in the container. When the container is full of popcorn, plan a popcorn party. What a tasteful way to encourage positive interactions between students!

Stella Levy—Gr. 3
Hackley School
Tarrytown, NY

Good-Behavior Coupons

Encourage outstanding student behavior with this weekly incentive program. Label a supply of paper rectangles with a variety of rewards and/or privileges. Place the resulting coupons in a decorated container. At the end of each week, invite every student who has displayed outstanding behavior during the week to draw a coupon from the container. Students can immediately redeem the coupons or they can save them for later use. In no time at all, you'll have a class of well-behaved coupon collectors!

Ann Southerland—Gr. 2, James Bowie Elementary, Midland, TX

Lonnie,
    Thanks for helping Stacy find her lunch money.
            Ms. Fischer

Notes of Praise

Boost your youngsters' self-esteem and encourage positive behavior with these simple notes of praise. Keep a supply of Post-it notes handy throughout the day. Each time a youngster exhibits praiseworthy behavior, note his actions on a Post-it note. When your students leave the room for recess or a special activity, attach the notes to the appropriate desks.

Christine Fischer—Special Education
George J. Peters School
Cranston, RI

Crackerjacks

Encourage students to reward their peers with crackerjack awards. When a child is chosen to be a classroom, bathroom, or lunchroom monitor, have him identify classmates displaying exemplary behavior. Then have the monitor report the crackerjack students to you. Write each crackerjack's name on an award and place the award in a box. At the end of the week, draw one child's award from the box, and present that child with a special prize or privilege. Return the remaining awards to the appropriate children.

Stephanie Miller—Gr. 2
Benefield Elementary
Lawrenceville, GA

Crackerjack Kid!

Great job, Jeff!

Date: _6-4-03_ From: _Ms. Miller_

Choosing Rewards

Students are motivated to do their best when they choose their own rewards. At the beginning of the year, give each student an index card. Have him write or dictate five rewards that he would like to receive. Rewards might include a few minutes of free time, writing on the chalkboard with colored chalk, or choosing a song for the class to sing. File the cards in a file box. When a student earns a reward, pull his card from the box and treat him to one of his chosen rewards.

Linette Farris, John C. French Elementary School, Cuero, TX

Good Behavior Tickets

Cite positive behaviors with tickets—raffle tickets, that is! Cut a supply of construction paper tickets or use tickets from a preprinted roll. Each time a student demonstrates a positive behavior, award him a ticket. Have students personalize their tickets before dropping them into a designated container. Periodically draw a ticket from the container and award its owner a special prize or privilege. "And the winner is..."

Cathy Cavasos—Gr. 2
Hickok School
Ulysses, KS

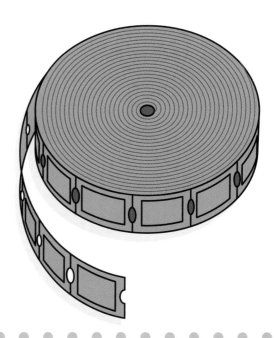

Good Behavior

Tidy Desks

An element of mystery makes this clean desk incentive extra rewarding! Prepare five small signs like the one shown and attach a strip of magnetic tape to the back of each one. Begin each week by reminding the class that five desks are being monitored for neatness; however, do not reveal which five. At the end of the week, secretly secure a prepared sign under each of the five desks that were kept orderly throughout the week. When the signs are discovered, reward each honoree with a sticker or a small treat.

Misty Rios—Gr. 2
Ward Elementary
Downey, CA

Thank-You List

Honor students for positive behavior and good citizenship with this satisfying, yet inexpensive reward. Write the words *Thank You* on a section of your chalkboard. As students exhibit notable behavior, write their names on the board. At the end of the day, thank these students with handshakes and/or hugs.

Kathleen Hunter—Gr. 2, Tara Elementary, Forest Park, GA

Visits From the Desk Fairy

Promote reading as you motivate students to keep neat-as-a-pin desks! Create a supply of duplicated notes from the Desk Fairy similar to the ones shown. Attach a small sticker or another treat to each one. When the students are out of the room, slip a note from the Desk Fairy into each neatly organized student desk. Once the word gets out, youngsters will eagerly keep tidy desks in anticipation of the Desk Fairy's next visit!

Bonnie Lanterman
Armstrong Elementary School
Hazelwood, MO

Monstrously Good Manners

Looking for a quick and easy way to improve classroom manners? Try using monster magnets with your students. To make monster magnets, cut a desired number of circle shapes from a piece of oaktag. Print "Monstrously Good Manners" on each oaktag circle; then decorate each one with a picture of a monster. Laminate the circles for durability; then attach a piece of magnetic tape to the back of each one. When you see a student using good manners, stick a magnet to the metallic portion of his desk. With this incentive, classroom manners will improve in no time at all.

Lisa Dorsey—Gr. 2, Heather Glen Elementary, Garland, TX

Reward-Winning Restaurant

When you're ready to reward hardworking or well-behaved students, invite them out to lunch! Don't worry; you won't have to go far to find a suitable restaurant. Your own classroom will do nicely. On the day of the special lunch, decorate a table with a fancy tablecloth and a centerpiece. Play soft background music and provide dessert if desired. Students will enjoy eating their lunches in style. Who knows? You might even earn a four-star rating for your charming classroom cafe.

Marilyn Cameron—Gr. 3
Gray Elementary
Houston, TX

Pizza by the Slice

Reinforce fractions and motivate students to be on their best behavior! Draw a pizza shape on the chalkboard; then divide it into six or more equal slices. Each time you observe exemplary behavior, reward the class by coloring one pizza slice. Also announce the fraction that tells how much pizza is colored and write it near the pie. When the entire pizza is decorated, reward the class with a tasty snack of pizza-flavored Goldfish crackers. Then erase the toppings, reslice the pizza, and repeat the process. Yum!

Dawn Scott—Gr. 2
Baxter Elementary
Midlothian, TX

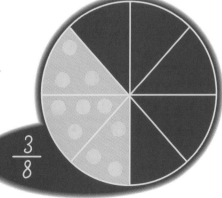

Good Behavior

Positive Sticks

This positive approach motivates students to stick with good behavior! Decorate one clean, empty juice can for each group of student desks. Each time you observe a group of students displaying outstanding behavior, place a craft stick in its container. At the end of the day, have the class give the group that earned the most sticks a standing ovation!

Julie Simpson—Gr. 2
Cherry Elementary
Toledo, OH

Brownie Points

This tasty incentive program motivates youngsters to be the best that they can be. With your students' help, create a list of positive behaviors and/or academic challenges that exceed the established expectations. Assign a point value to each item on the list; then display the list in a prominent classroom location. For added visual appeal, shape a border from aluminum foil to resemble a baking pan. Create a chart on which to record the points the class earns each day. When the class earns a predetermined number of points, reward the students with a freshly baked pan of brownies. If desired, enlist your students' help in making the treat. No doubt these will be the tastiest brownie points your students have ever earned!

Brenda Martin—Grs. 2–3, Baty Elementary School, Del Valle, TX

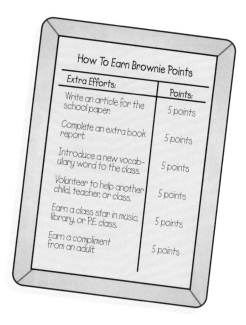

How To Earn Brownie Points	
Extra Efforts:	**Points:**
Write an article for the school paper.	5 points
Complete an extra book report.	5 points
Introduce a new vocabulary word to the class.	5 points
Volunteer to help another child, teacher, or class.	5 points
Earn a class star in music, library, or P.E. class.	5 points
Earn a compliment from an adult.	5 points

That was great!
Mr. Reiffenberger

Getting Along With Others

Make recess duty a positive experience by rewarding good citizenship. Duplicate several certificates with messages such as "Thanks! I really like what you did!" and "That was great!" Attach stickers or fast-food coupons to the certificates and award them to well-mannered youngsters.

Don Reiffenberger—Gr. 3
Laura B. Anderson Elementary
Sioux Falls, SD

Flying High!

Promoting Good Behaviors

Encourage outstanding student behavior with a minimal amount of teacher preparation. Mount an open worksheet (like the one shown) on construction paper; then display the resulting incentive chart in a convenient location. Each time students are observed demonstrating positive behaviors, color a space on the chart. When all of the spaces are colored, reward the students with small individual prizes or a class privilege. If desired have a drawing to determine which student takes home the colorful chart. Repeat the procedure as frequently as desired.

Kathy Quinlan—Gr. 2, Charles E. Bennett Elementary
Green Cove Springs, FL

Flipping Chips

Hit the jackpot with good behavior! Arrange students' desks in tables; then place a small basket in the center of each table. Fill your pockets with game chips. Throughout the day, when you see the students at a table displaying desired behaviors, flip a chip into their basket. At the end of the day, have each group count its chips and record them on a class graph. Set a class goal for the week. If the goal is met, reward the class with a special privilege. With this cooperative approach, everyone is a winner!

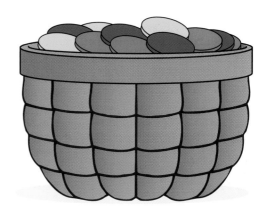

Linda Luiser—Gr. 3, Boggy Creek Elementary, Kissimmee, FL

Good Behavior Poster

Reinforce positive classroom behavior with this exciting puzzle activity. Mount an eye-catching poster onto tagboard and laminate it. Also laminate a blank piece of tagboard of equal size. Cut the blank piece of tagboard into puzzle pieces and number each piece. Then assemble the numbered pieces atop the poster, attaching each piece with two-sided tape or rubber cement. Display the poster puzzle at the front of your room. Throughout the day, allow students displaying positive behaviors to remove pieces of the puzzle and guess what is on the poster. Reward the child who guesses correctly with a small prize. Your students will be so eager to participate, they'll dazzle you with great behavior.

Diane L. Lucas, Northern Area Elementary School, Pittsburgh, PA

Good Behavior

Table Management Tool

Here's a great management idea to use when your students are working at tables. Number each table and color-code each student's table space. Refer to table numbers when praising groups of students who are exhibiting positive behaviors. When it is time to tidy up, call out a color. All students who are represented by the color chosen are responsible for cleanup duty. Your room will be spiffy in a jiffy!

Mae Purrenhage—Grs. 3–5
Jackson Elementary
Fort Campbell, KY

Good Manners Detective

Enlist your students' help in recognizing and encouraging good manners. Each morning remind students to be on the lookout for good manners. At the end of the day, ask students to recall instances in which their classmates exhibited good manners; then invite one student to tell the class about the good manners that she saw being practiced. Afterward have her announce the names of the students she thought were particularly well mannered. Thanks to this great idea, your students will soon come to expect from themselves the same good manners they are looking for in each other.

Kathleen Ann Weisenborn—Gr. 2, Fricano Elementary School, Lockport, NY

Egg Incentives

Encourage positive behavior and good work habits with this seasonal approach. Fill a basket with plastic eggs, one per student. Every morning have each student take a plastic egg. Each student attempts to keep his egg until the end of the school day by displaying positive behavior and good work habits. If a student behaves inappropriately, his egg must be returned to the basket. At the end of the day, have those students who have kept their eggs personalize slips of paper; then place the papers and the eggs in the basket. Each Friday afternoon draw one name from the basket. Present the winning student with a special sticker, bookmark, or poster.

Sue Volk
Newton, IL

Special Person of the Day

Spotlight a different youngster each day of the month with this special calendar display. First, program a blank calendar grid with the dates for the month. Next, personalize the squares that represent school days with student names. On her designated day, a student illustrates her square and becomes your special helper for the day. It's a great way to foster self-esteem and reinforce calendar skills.

Carol Baird
Johns Hopkins Avenue Elementary School
Jackson, MS

SEPTEMBER

S	M	T	W	T	F	S
		Donald 1	Tomeka 2	Alicia 3	Bettina 4	5
6	Labor Day 7	Crystal 8	Adam 9	Diane 10	JeKara 11	12

Roll Out the Red Carpet

Students feel like royalty when they receive the red-carpet treatment for personal successes. Place a square of red carpet underneath the desk of each student who demonstrated outstanding behavior or academic progress the previous school day. Present each student with a red certificate from page 181 that entitles him to a specified number of rewards and/or privileges throughout the day of his reign. Though each student steps down from his throne when the day is done, his positive feelings about himself will have just begun.

Margie Siegel—Gr. 2, Wren Hollow Elementary, Ballwin, MO

Today Samuel Crump
Received the
Red Carpet
Treatment

Good-Behavior Stamp Books

Encourage outstanding student behavior with this easy-to-manage incentive program. You will need some colorful stamp pads, a variety of rubber stamps, and one stamp-collection booklet per child. To make a booklet like the one shown, staple sheets of recycled paper atop a slightly larger sheet of construction paper. Have students display their booklets atop their desks at all times. Each time you observe a student demonstrating positive behavior, stamp the top page of her booklet. When a child earns a predetermined number of stamps, she may exchange the booklet page for a special prize or privilege. For added motivation, occasionally declare a Double-Stamp Day.

Beth Davino, Acreage Lines Elementary
West Palm Beach, FL

Good Behavior

Stop to Think

Lesson the time needed to settle down students who have had an argument. When a disagreement surfaces, separate the youngsters and ask each one to complete a copy of the form on page 182. By the time the forms are complete, students will have calmed down and thought through the incident, and will perhaps be more willing to consider other perspectives. Review the situation with the students involved, determine the consequences, and then have the students sign the forms. File the forms to use as a reference during parent communications.

Ellie Guldan—Guidance Counselor
Eaton Elementary School
Lenoir City, TN

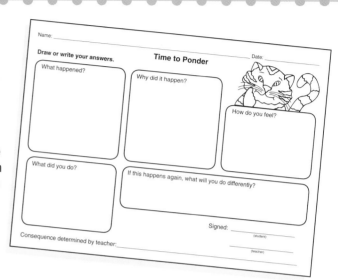

Name: _____

Draw or write your answers.   **Time to Ponder**   Date: _____

What happened?

Why did it happen?

How do you feel?

What did you do?

If this happens again, what will you do differently?

Signed: _____
(student)

Consequence determined by teacher: _____
(teacher)

Time to Think

Use this behavior plan and turn negative situations into positive learning experiences. Position a Think About It desk in a quiet area of the classroom. When a child displays inappropriate behavior, ask her to sit at the Think About It desk. Challenge the child to contemplate her behavior and decide what she should have done differently. After a few minutes, meet with the youngster to discuss the situation, determine an appropriate behavior, and, if necessary, agree upon a suitable consequence. This problem-solving approach to behavior management has lasting effects.

Sandra L. Carpenter, Litchfield Elementary School, Litchfield Park, AZ

The End-of-the-Day Box

If your students' small toys seem to appear at inappropriate times, try this safekeeping system. Cover a shoebox with Con-Tact paper; then label it with a pattern (page 183). Program the clock-face cutout with your dismissal time. If a student is playing with a toy during an inappropriate time, ask him to put it in the End-of-the-Day Box. The box will safely hold your students' treasures until the end of the day.

Bernadette Carnevale
Buffalo, NY

THE END-OF-THE-DAY BOX

Passports to Success

Keep youngsters motivated through the year with passports to success. Explain to students that the school year is similar to an extended trip: they will see, experience, and learn many new things. Next, ask each youngster to set two goals for himself. One or both goals may be school related. Then have students copy their goals on duplicate passports similar to the one shown. Explain that these goals will be a monthlong journey for them. After one month have each youngster evaluate his goals. If a student meets a goal, he earns a stamp on his passport. If a student does not meet a goal, help him evaluate and rewrite that goal in his next month's passport. At the end of the year, students will have "traveled" quite a distance, and they'll have a passport to prove it!

Ana Maria B. Lewis—Gr. 3
Crosby Elementary School
Harrison, OH

Organizing Daily Work

My students organize their daily work in file folders bearing mailboxes. At the end of the day the folders are turned in. If a student has completed his work satisfactorily, he earns a tally mark in his mailbox. When a student has received ten tally marks, he earns a sticker or a special privilege. These folders are handy tools for monitoring complete work. And my students can see the progress they are making.

Linda Borchering
J. Colin English Elementary School
North Fort Myers, FL

Cursive Champs

Once the newness of cursive writing wears off, the quality of students' cursive penmanship often suffers. To maintain high-quality cursive penmanship, use the punch card and the coupon on page 184. First, give each student a Cursive Champ punch card. Each time a student demonstrates quality cursive writing on his assignments, he earns a punch on his card. When his punch card is completely punched, he turns it in for a coupon that entitles him to complete one assignment of his choice using manuscript writing. This small incentive really helps maintain high-quality penmanship on daily assignments.

Tanya Wilder—Gr. 3
Wolf Creek Elementary
Broken Arrow, OK

Work Habits

Bingo Card Rewards

Keep track of students' good work with blank bingo cards. Give each child a card. Each day the child completes his work satisfactorily, allow him to draw an X in one square on his card. When the card is filled, let the student reach into a prize bucket for a prize.

Martha Alfrey
Rose Hill Christian School
Ironton, OH

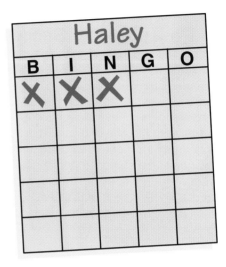

Self-Esteem Stamps

My rubber stamp collection has grown over the years. Selecting a stamp to use on good work is fun. Passing this honor on to the students has done wonders for neatness in our class.

When we start an assignment, I announce that one student will get to choose the stamp I will award for this set of papers. The lucky student will be a quiet, neat worker. I select the winner after everyone has completed the paper. The papers are beautiful, and the room is quiet.

Mary Dinneen
Bristol, CT

Promoting Quality Work

This incentive program motivates students to carefully complete their work. Each student needs a personalized punch card pattern (page 185). A student earns one punch for each perfect paper that she completes. (For easy management, post the times during which you are available to punch students' cards.) When all of the punches on a child's card have been removed, she exchanges her card for a new one and receives a small prize. If desired, compile your youngsters' completed punch cards on a shower ring. When 50 cards have been collected, reward the entire class with a special treat or privilege.

Judy Janzen—Gr. 3
Joshua Independent School District
Joshua, TX

Paper of the Day!

Paper of the Day

Encourage students to carefully complete their work with this paper-of-the-day plan. Conclude each day by presenting one outstanding assignment that was completed that day. Enlist your students' help in identifying the positive qualities of the paper, such as neatness, accuracy, originality, and completeness. Then showcase the paper in a special frame designed for this purpose. A round of applause for the proud owner of the paper of the day is definitely in order!

Debbie Byrne
Candor Elementary
Candor, NY

Secret-Agent Numbers

Reinforce problem-solving strategies and minimize interruptions with this management plan. Number a set of secret-agent cards (one per student) and numerically stack the cards on top of your desk. When a student feels that she needs your assistance, but you are working with a small group or an individual, she takes a card. Her mission is to answer her question independently or with the help of another available classmate. As time permits, sequentially call the numbers that have been taken from the card stack. Congratulate those youngsters who successfully solved their own cases, and help those students who need your assistance.

Susan Pomfred—Gr. 2, Green Meadow School, Maynard, MA

Picturing Student Progress

Are you often left wondering how many students are still working on a project or special assignment? This kid-pleasing approach gives you a clear picture of your students' progress. Draw an object or character on the chalkboard. As each student completes his work, he draws a designated figure near the drawing. A glance at the chalkboard indicates how many students have completed the assignment. The drawing also serves as a visual reminder for students to finish their work.

Sr. Helen Theresa
Incarnation School
Trenton, MA

Stamps of Approval

Use a holiday rubber stamp collection as an incentive for students to finish their work. Assign a stamp and ink color for work to be done for each day. As students turn in completed work, each child stamps her right or left hand using the assigned color and stamp. Children love to be stamped, and by a glance you can tell who has completed what!

Kaen Bellis
Stover, MO

Homework Excuses

Keeping a personalized record of homework excuses encourages students to turn in their homework on time. In a spiral notebook, personalize one page per student. When a student has an incomplete or forgotten homework assignment, enter the date and the assignment on his page in the notebook. Beneath the entry, have the student write why he was unable to turn in his homework as assigned. The "excuse book" makes students accountable for their homework, and it provides excellent documentation when conferring with students and their parents. You're sure to get some unusual excuses, but fewer and fewer students will be forgetting their homework!

Susan Shaw, Gr. 2, John Baker Elementary School, Albuquerque, NM

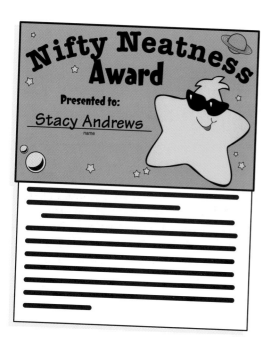

Nifty Neatness Awards

I use Nifty Neatness Awards to encourage neat work in my class. Students know that each day (or every other day), one assignment is eligible for Nifty Neatness Awards (page 186)—but they aren't sure which one. I secretly choose one set of papers from all of the assignments I collect. Each student who completes that assignment neatly is awarded a neatness certificate, which I staple to the top of his paper. When papers are returned, students remove their awards and save them. After earning ten awards, a student is eligible for one of a variety of privileges such as skipping an assignment, being the teacher's helper for the day, or having extra free time.

Dianne Neumann—Gr. 2
Frank C. Whiteley School
Hoffman Estates, IL

Color-Coded Flowerpots

These one-of-a-kind flowerpots are a fun way to color-code groups of students' desks (or tables). Use a different color of paint to decorate an inexpensive plastic flowerpot for each group. Also make several like-colored tissue paper flowers for each pot. Tape each flower to one end of a wooden skewer or a green pipe cleaner and attach construction paper leaves to the resulting stems. When the painted pots are dry, put a layer of rocks in the bottom of each one (for added weight). Trim a piece of florist's foam to fit inside each pot; then press the foam in place and poke the flower stems into the foam. Present each group of students with a pot-o'-blooms. "Just look at that yellow group! Each of its members are ready to begin."

Marie Lain
Marjory Stoneman Douglas Elementary
Miami, FL

Swap and Check

Use this class activity to reinforce your youngsters' proofreading skills. Periodically, before students hand in their completed assignments, have them swap papers with their classmates. Instruct students to proofread their classmates' work and indicate any corrections that need to be made. After a predetermined amount of time, have papers returned to their owners. Each student then evaluates his paper and makes the needed corrections.

Mary Dinneen, Mountain View School, Bristol, CT

Row 1: ||||| ||

Row 2: |||||

Row 3: ||||| |||

Following Directions Tally

This behavior modification system reinforces following directions. Number each row or table of students; then list the numbers on the chalkboard. After delivering oral directions to the whole class, observe each team of students. Draw a tally mark beside the number of each team that followed directions promptly and appropriately. Continue this procedure for two weeks. Then, as a large-group activity, tally each team's marks. Reward the team that has the most marks with a special privilege or individual treats.

Phyllis Kidder
Okinawa, Japan

Work Habits

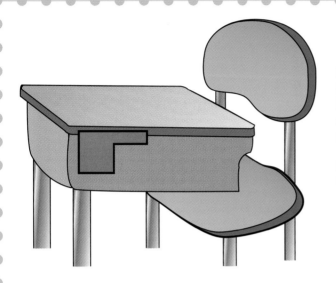

Silent Signal

Monitoring independent workers just got easier! For each student, laminate a red poster board flag like the one shown and use a Velcro fastener to attach it horizontally to the side of his desk. When a youngster needs assistance, he alerts you by turning his flag upright. Now there's an idea that really delivers!

Michele Curlings
Oak Grove Elementary School

Ask Three Before You Ask Me

Put a familiar phrase to good use as students take responsibility for their own learning. Post the phrase "Ask Three Before You Ask Me" in a prominent location as a reminder for students. Tell your youngsters that if they have a question, they should ask three other students before asking you. Before a child asks you a question, have him name the three students he's already asked. Students will create an atmosphere of cooperation, and you'll minimize the number of times you repeat directions!

Cheryl A. Wade—Gr. 2, Golden Springs Elementary, Oxford, AL

A Penny Earned

Earning and learning go hand in hand with this simple classroom management technique. Each Monday tape a strip of five paper coins to each student's desk. To earn a coin each day, a student must satisfactorily complete her assignments for the day and have her coin initialed by you. Before dismissal on Friday, have each child cut out her earned coins and place them in her personal piggy bank (a resealable plastic bag labeled with her name) and then return any unearned coins to you. At the end of each grading period, plan a celebratory snack. Design a menu that lists snack items—such as apples, oranges, popcorn, cookies, and juice—with their corresponding prices. Students use the coins they've earned to purchase the snacks of their choice. In addition to learning the value of using time wisely, students experience practical applications of their math skills.

Cheryl Gjesvold—Resource
Fairfield Elementary
Fairfield, MT

Patterns

Use the license and coupon patterns with "Driver's License" on page 146.

Week One

Week Two

Name_____ Date_____

Good behavior is the rule of the road!

©The Education Center, Inc. • *500 Classroom Tips* • TEC60848

Week Four

Week Three

©The Education Center, Inc. • *500 Classroom Tips* • TEC60848

Gotcha
being good!

 # Gotcha
being good!

Gotcha
being good!

 # Gotcha
being good!

Gotcha
being good!

Terrific News!

To: _____

From: _____

TERRIFIC NEWS!

TO: _____

FROM: _____

Weekly Update

Name: _____

☐ = Outstanding ☐ = Needs Practice ☐ = Satisfactory	Week Of:								
Listens Carefully									
Stay on Task									
Follows Directions									
Treats Others With Respect									
Follows Class Rules									
Does His/Her Best Work									
Parent's Initials									

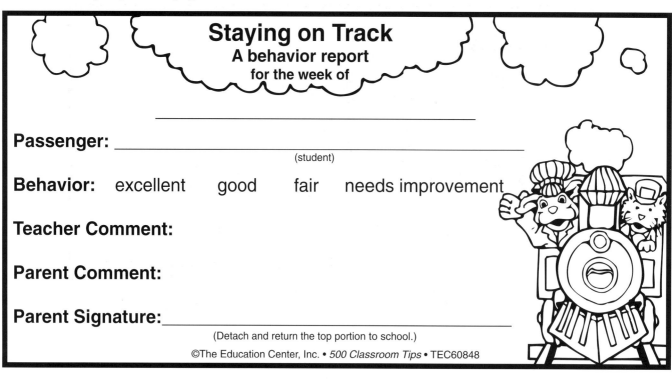

Staying on Track
A behavior report
for the week of

_____

Passenger: _____
(student)

Behavior: excellent   good   fair   needs improvement

Teacher Comment:

Parent Comment:

Parent Signature: _____

(Detach and return the top portion to school.)

©The Education Center, Inc. • *500 Classroom Tips* • TEC60848

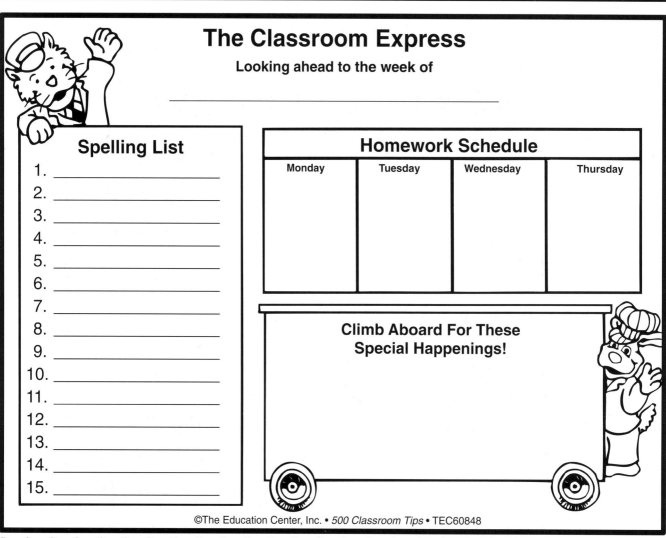

The Classroom Express
Looking ahead to the week of

_____

Spelling List
1. _____
2. _____
3. _____
4. _____
5. _____
6. _____
7. _____
8. _____
9. _____
10. _____
11. _____
12. _____
13. _____
14. _____
15. _____

Homework Schedule

Monday	Tuesday	Wednesday	Thursday

Climb Aboard For These Special Happenings!

©The Education Center, Inc. • *500 Classroom Tips* • TEC60848

Today _____

Received the

Red Carpet

Treatment

©The Education Center, Inc. • *500 Classroom Tips* • TEC60848

Today _____

Received the

Red Carpet

Treatment

©The Education Center, Inc. • *500 Classroom Tips* • TEC60848

Today _____

Received the

Red Carpet

Treatment

©The Education Center, Inc. • *500 Classroom Tips* • TEC60848

Name: _____

Date: _____

Time to Ponder

Draw or write your answers.

What happened?

Why did it happen?

How do you feel?

What did you do?

If this happens again, what will you do differently?

Consequence determined by teacher: _____

Signed: _____
(student)

_____
(teacher)

©The Education Center, Inc. • *500 Classroom Tips* • TEC60848

Note to the teacher: Use with "Stop to Think" on page 170.

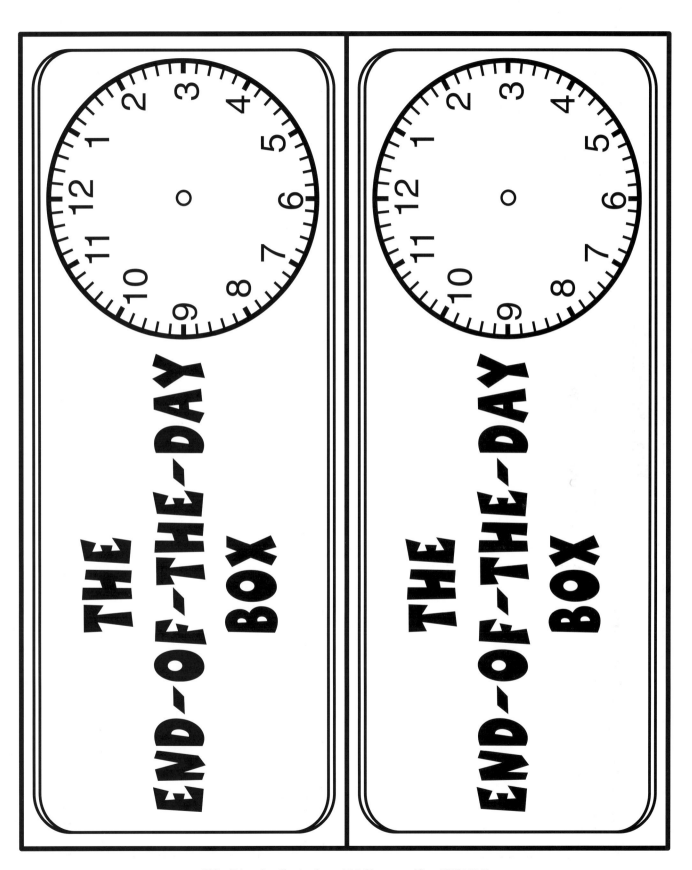

Cursive Champ

_____
name

This coupon entitles

_____
name

to complete an assignment using manuscript writing.

Cursive Champ

_____
name

This coupon entitles

_____
name

to complete an assignment using manuscript writing.

Punch Card

Presented to:

_____
name

©The Education Center, Inc. • *500 Classroom Tips* • TEC60848

Presented to:

_____
name

©The Education Center, Inc. • *500 Classroom Tips* • TEC60848

Communications

Contents

Parent

Charting a Course Toward Better Communication

Maintain a record of positive parent-teacher communications with this handy chart. On a sheet of paper, list your students' names in a column to the left. Draw lines to make three or more additional columns. Label the columns with headings such as "Phone Call," "Good News Gram," "Postcard," and "Personal Contact." Each time you have positive communication with a parent about his or her child, note the date and the reason for the contact in the appropriate column on the chart. A quick glance at the chart reveals who needs to hear from you next! Make a new chart at the beginning of each grading period.

Kristyn Haberkorn—Gr. 2
Greenvale Park Elementary
Northfield, MN

Positive Parent-Teacher Communications

Student	Phone Call	Good News Gram	Postcard	Personal Contact
Beatrice		12/8 Timed Test		1/4 Science Quiz
Cathy	12/5 Behavior		1/9 Homework	

Files at Your Fingertips

How often do you momentarily misplace notes from parents because they accidentally become buried under other school-related paperwork? This easy filing system can put a stop to these frightful moments. Label a hanging file folder for each student; then place the folders in a hanging file box that you have positioned within an arm's reach of your desk. When a student hands you a note from her parent(s), read the note; then immediately place it in the student's file. If you need to retrieve the note, you'll know right where to find it.

Leslee McWhirter
Mendel Elementary
Houston, TX

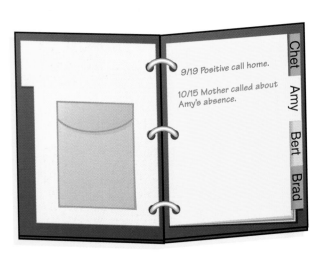

9/19 Positive call home.

10/15 Mother called about Amy's absence.

Organizing Correspondence

Keep parent correspondence at your fingertips! Label a tab divider for each child. Tape a 6" x 9" envelope to the back of each divider and then alphabetize the dividers and place them in a three-ring binder. Store correspondence in the envelope and log phone communications on the divider. Nifty!

Monnette Tyner—Gr. 3, Houston Elementary, Mineral Wells, TX

Calling All Parents

Children are notorious for placing in their pockets important papers which are never again seen in recognizable form. To make sure vital information is being received by parents, laminate a class set of manila envelopes like the one shown. Inform parents that papers requiring immediate attention will be carried home in these envelopes. Also include in each envelope a checklist that indicates what actions need to be taken and, if desired, a receipt form to be signed and returned in the envelope the following day. This system keeps parents and teachers informed!

Susanna Zumbro & Maggie Griffin
Britt Elementary
Snellville, GA

Subject Displays

Give parents a clear picture of what their youngsters are learning with these student-made displays. Assign a group of students to each area; then ask each group to creatively create a display that reflects what has been or is being learned in its assigned subject area. Encourage students to use a variety of visual aids such as charts, posters, maps, and filmstrips. Audio aids can also be included. Exhibit the eye-catching displays around the classroom. Now that's impressive!

Jill Raveling—Gr. 3, Rudd Elementary, New Waverly, TX

Pocketing Papers

Help students organize take-home papers with pocket folders. Personalize and label a two-pocket folder for each child. Ask students to store the folders in their desks during the day and take the folders home each afternoon. Whenever you distribute items that are to be taken home (graded papers, announcements, notes to parents), designate in which folder pocket each item should be placed. Parents can quickly see which papers are to be kept, and which ones need to be read and returned to school in the folder. Parents will appreciate this organized approach, and you'll spend less time tracking down missing correspondence.

Bernadette Burns
High Bridge Elementary School
High Bridge, NJ

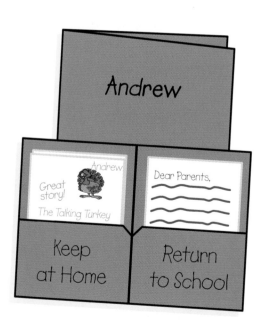

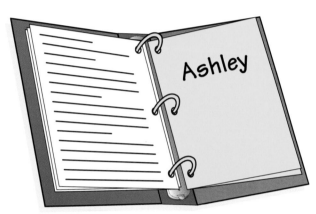

Keeping Up With Correspondence

Managing parent correspondence can seem like a full-time job. Make the task easier with this handy parent communication binder. Purchase a large three-ring binder and a class supply of pocket dividers. Label one pocket for each student. Also complete a student information sheet for each child. Place each child's information sheet and pocket folder side by side in your binder. Each time you receive a written message from a parent, file it in the appropriate pocket. And if you wish to respond to a parent, the information you need is right at your fingertips.

Anna Kellum—Gr. 2
Forest Hills Elementary, Walterboro, SC

Student Information Notebook

Record important student information and document parent communications in this one-of-a-kind notebook. On individual pages in a spiral notebook, write your students' names in alphabetical order. Allow one or more blank pages between each entry. On each personalized page, list the student's date of birth, home address, and home phone number. Also list the name of each parent and a daytime phone number where he or she can be reached. If desired, list an emergency contact person and note any allergies the student may have. Throughout the year, record all parent communications in the notebook. List the date, the time, and a brief description of the communication (phone call, written note, conference). Record the nature and outcome of each contact. This thorough method of documentation becomes a great reference throughout the year.

MaryAnne Marshall, Orange, NJ

Wristband Reminders

Remind students and parents of upcoming events with wristband reminders. Keep a supply of 8½" x 1" paper strips on hand. When you wish to send a reminder home, write the desired message on the chalkboard and have each student copy the message onto a paper strip. Ask each child to wrap his resulting reminder around his wrist so that you can tape or staple the ends of the strip together. These nifty reminders are the perfect fit for any occasion!

Tara Murphy
Oconee County Primary School
Watkinsville, GA

Field trip tomorrow. Bring your lunch.

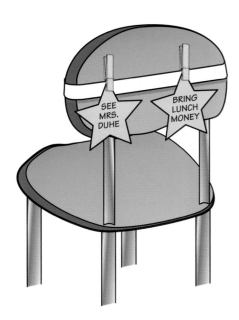

Student Memo Line

Here's an easy way to relay a message to your students. Make a memo line for each student by tying a length of elastic around his chair. Make copies of the messages you use most often; then laminate them for durability. Use a clothespin to attach an appropriate message to a student's memo line. After the student takes care of the matter pinned on his memo line, he removes the message and returns it to you.

Kathleen R. Duhe—Gr. 3
St. Amant Elementary School
St. Amant, LA

Personal Mailboxes

I provide a personal mailbox for each of my students by attaching press-on pockets to their desks. When papers or notes need to be distributed, I put them in the students' mailboxes. I also have a mailbox attached to my desk. It's a nice catchall for notes and drawings addressed to me.

Tara Murphy, Oconee County Primary School, Watkinsville, GA

Silent Echoes

Wish you could keep a lid on echoed responses like "That was my answer!" and "I was going to say that too!" without discouraging student participation? Here's the perfect solution! Show students how to sign the phrase "Me too" in sign language. This is done by signing the letter y (see inset), and then, with your palm facing down and your thumb pointed toward your chest, moving your hand back and forth horizontally as shown. When you see students signing "Me too," acknowledge their response with a phrase like "I see several of you agree with Matthew." You'll have plenty of student participation and minimal interruptions.

Cheryl Phillips—Substitute Teacher
Baltimore, MD

Fantastic Folders

Help your youngsters organize their papers with this simple pocket-folder system. Have each student bring three pocket folders to school. Collect one of the folders and store it as a replacement. Have each student label one folder "Stay at School" and decorate it and label another folder "Take Home" and decorate it. Explain to your students that schoolwork for collection at the end of each day should be placed in their "Stay at School" folders. Papers that need to be taken home should be placed in their "Take Home" folders for review with a parent each night. (You may choose to include a parent sign-off sheet in each "Take Home" folder.) Parents and students will agree—this organized approach is fantastic!

Margie Siegel—Gr. 2
Wren Hollow Elementary School
Ballwin, MO

Completing Work

Student numbers and two-pocket folders will help you identify which students have not turned in an assignment. Label a two-pocket folder for each subject area. Inside each folder, label one pocket "Numbers 1–20" and the other "Numbers 13–25."(Adjust the numbers to fit your class size.) Next assign each student a number based on an alphabetical class list. Have students write their assigned numbers in the top right-hand corners of their papers. As students complete their work, they locate the appropriate subject folder and numerically file their papers. To determine who has not turned in an assignment, flip through the pages in each folder and note which ones are missing. Write an assignment and the missing student numbers on the chalkboard as a reminder of who needs to turn in work.

Marcie McDuffie—Gr. 3
Huddleston Elementary School
Peachtree City, GA

Taking Papers Home

Save precious class time by sending home corrected student work once a week. Have each child personalize the front of a file folder. Laminate the folders for durability and tape a parent response sheet, like the one shown, inside each one. Once a week, set aside a few minutes to distribute the folders and your students' corrected work. Each child carries his papers home inside his folder. A parent removes and reviews the contents of the folder; then he or she dates, signs, and adds a comment to the response sheet. The following school day, the student returns the empty folder. Each week you'll save time and communicate with parents!

Tomara Steadman, St. Marks Elementary, Colwich, KS